Jumbo Arrow-words

100 puzzles

Book 1

Published by Richardson Publishing Group Limited
www.richardsonpublishinggroup.com

10 9 8 7 6 5 4 3 2 1

All puzzles supplied by Clarity Media

Cover design by Junior London

ISBN 978-1-913602-21-5

Printed and bound by Bell & Bain Ltd, 303 Burnfield Road, Thornliebank, Glasgow G46 7UQ

A catalogue record for this book is available from the British Library.

If you would like to comment on any aspect of this book, please contact us at:

E-mail: puzzles@richardsonpublishinggroup.com

Follow us on Twitter @puzzlesandgames
instagram.com/richardsonpuzzlesandgames
facebook.com/richardsonpuzzlesandgames

Contents

Instructions

Simply answer the clues in the direction each of the arrows point to fill the crossword-style grid.

No. 1

- Health resort
- Failure to understand
- Jamaican style of music
- Defer action
- Not as clear
- ___ Titmuss: TV personality
- Made to order (6-5)
- Unique product feature (inits)
- Introverted
- Locale of a famous leaning tower
- Calculating machine
- Woody plant
- Rating
- Feline animal
- Small boat
- Guessing game for children (1,3)
- Pack down tightly
- Some small batteries (abbr)
- Unmixed
- Woman's first public appearance (informal)
- Strip of leather worn round the waist
- Scarf of feathers or fur
- Chanted
- Mineral deposit
- ___-Wan Kenobi: Star Wars character
- Character in The Simpsons
- Part of a curve
- Yellow citrus fruit
- Orderly grouping
- Computer operating system
- Item used in cricket
- Prophet
- President Lincoln (for short)
- ___ Gardner: US actress
- Russian country house
- ___ Maria: prayer
- Bravo
- Rough shelter (4-2)
- Eg from Montreal
- Fruit
- Aquatic mollusc
- Aunt ___: Bambi character
- Demanded
- Cobras
- Pickup vehicle in Australia
- Eleventh month (abbr)
- Organ of sight
- Cereal plant
- Unit of thermal resistance
- Cuddle
- Bite sharply
- Dig out of the ground
- Leo ___: War and Peace author
- Thee
- Single in number
- First woman
- Good ___: nice person

No. 2

Boxing class		Eg shellfish	Inn	Large deer (pl)	Code signal of distress (inits)	Large wading bird		Raised a question		Military equipment	Performer of an action
Remains of a fire						Uncovered					
New word or phrase										Measures duration	
Things to be done						Move on ice					
Backs of boats					Knife		Title of a Muslim ruler				
Bartender in The Simpsons				Bicycle for two people							Study (anag)
Predatory canine mammal					Mark left from a wound		Very small amount	___ Beatty: US actor			
			Make a choice	Massage technique							
Primary colour		Guards		Business leader (inits)				___ Musk: SpaceX founder	Russian space station	Parent / teacher group (inits)	
Economic stat. for a country (inits)				Try							
Opposite of cold				The world as it is							
			Snake-like fish	Great Lake of North America	Negligent	Narrow cut or opening	Rita ___: British singer				Smallest pig of the litter
Letters at the end of page one (inits)	Staggers						Not wet		Bleat of a sheep	___ Harding: Welsh actor	
Green gemstone								___ Cantrell: US R&B singer			
Thick; heavy	Cure-all							___ Rand: author			
					Cruel ruler						

No. 3

- Village People hit
- One who knows your thoughts (4,6)
- Assertion
- Seasons with sodium chloride
- Cruel or severe
- One (Spanish)
- Dwarfish creatures
- Enemy
- Makes better
- Victor ___: French poet and novelist
- Unstable massive stars (3,6)
- Group of two people
- Poorly behaved; impolite (3-8)
- ___ King Cole: US jazz pianist
- Friend of Tigger
- City on the River Ouse
- Flat circular plates
- Amide (anag)
- Scottish lake
- ___-haw: donkey sound
- Deity
- Limb
- Narrow strip of land
- Precipitate
- Increase in amount
- Mix; agitate
- Growing old
- Jacket
- African country
- Small batteries (abbr)
- Eg the 1990s
- Poker stake
- Spiny egg-laying mammal
- Five plus five
- To and ___: from place to place
- Refute by evidence
- ___ favor: please (Spanish)
- Direction opposite NNW
- Ancient boat
- Former term for euro
- ___ Rickman: English actor
- Engrossed
- Unpleasant monster
- Ridge of rock
- Organ of hearing
- Texter's digression (inits)
- Inflated feeling of pride
- Mythical monster
- Hit hard
- Command to a horse
- Pull at
- Tiny bird
- In the capacity of (formal)
- Isaac ___: physicist
- Young newt

No. 4

Desert plants	Relating to sound	Vineyard (in France)	Light brown colour		Metal container; element		Form of public transport	Topics for debate	Long mountain chain		Packaged ready for shipping
					Agreement or concord						
Seventh planet							One more than five				Haul
Horse shade				Pain or discomfort (informal)	Metallic element	Social isolation	Ooze				
Pirate's flag (5,5)		Water lily	Loose white judo jackets				Official language of Pakistan				
										Ice home	
Rodent	Gelatinous substance		___ Pot: Khmer Rouge leader				Travel on water				
			Portico in ancient Greece	Nothing (informal)				About 2.2 pounds (abbr)	Fearless and brave		Possess
___ Van Sant: US film director				Keep out	In good health		Was in first place				
								At this moment			
Prodigal		Nitrous ___: laughing gas						Heavy weight			
Jewel	Greek god of love	Performed on stage						Allot justice		Fish	Hens lay these
			Annual car test (inits)		Signal assent with the head	Expected at a certain time	Stomach muscles (informal)				
Circular hall								Breed of dog			
			Multiplying by two								
Small spot		Yields						___ Kapital: Karl Marx work			

No. 5

___ Falco: US actress

___ beetle: type of insect

Prologue (abbr)

___ Blair: US actress

Male bee

Word used to express disgust

Disposition

Athletic facility

Divisor

Moral obligation

Instructing

___ up: placed in position

Expansion

Cash dispenser (inits)

Unit of resistance

Female kangaroo

Instruct; teach

Long cloud of smoke

Former Italian currency

First woman

El ___: Spanish hero

17th Greek letter

___ McIlroy: Northern Irish golfer

Lhasa ___: dog breed

Japanese masked drama

Horse colour

Attrition (anag)

___ Grande: US singer

Regions

Tasteless items (informal)

Lethargy

Tubular pasta

Comes into collision with

Word expressing negation

___ Kilmer: famous actor

___ Els: golfer

Extra postscript (inits)

Canine warning sound

Your (poetic)

Fluffy scarf

Pop group whose hits include SOS

Catch sight of

Blow out air loudly

___ Pound: US poet

Bleat of a sheep

Sphere or globe

Navigation aid (abbr)

___ up: agitated

Elongated rectangles

Gun

Tear

Hairstyle of tight curls

Arrest

Superior of a nunnery

Cooling tool

No. 6

Uneasy
Dryness
City in central Spain
Level and regular
Relieve or free from
___ Redding: US singer
Cuts; trims
Wealthy and influential people
Fat used to make puddings

Male parent
Russian sovereigns

Supplying
Long for

Angered; irritated
From that time

Paradise garden
Criminal
Constituent

Removed from sight
Afternoon sleep
Flower

Public school
Helps
Knowledge (abbr)
___ Green: French actress

Id ___: that is to say
Assumed identities

Nay (anag)
Sentiment
___ McKellen: English actor
Typeface
Guitar with four strings (abbr)
Fasten with stitches

Things that may happen
Scatter widely

Animal doctor
Cue sport

Country that borders Iraq
___ Daly: TV presenter
Possesses
Long periods of history
Opposite of old
Tiny specks

Brett ___: Australian fast bowler
Supple
Female parent
Frying pan
Colour or tint

Gun
Doctor ___: TV show

Road information boards
Capital of the Bahamas
Opposite of in

Cooks in wood chippings

No. 7

Compel	Barack ___: former US President	Friend of Tigger	Young bear		Wetland		For what purpose	Son of Daedalus in Greek mythology	Princely		Storage place
					Applauded						
Springy							Kind of flat hat				Think or suppose
Final line on an agenda (inits)				Suffix for some image files	US state	Wearisome	Affirm solemnly				
Contrived		Item kept in a humidor	Stomach or belly				Religious act				
										Snow home	
Lively dance	Apple tablet		Not near				Cut of beef from the foreleg				
			Walk through water	___-haw: donkey sound				Cut down a tree	Definite and clear		Opposite of high
Animal foot				___ bells: orchestral instrument	Cooking appliance		Don (anag)				
								Sound of a cow			
Long foot race		Italian cathedral						Sound of a punch			
La ___: Bolivian city	Some small batteries (abbr)	Receded						Feeble (of an excuse)		Not stereo	___ bread: French toast
			Spot (informal)		Climbing plant	Dandy	Blue ___: bird				
Aerial rescue								Unit of thermal resistance			
			Evading								
Pet feline		Vault under a church						Bashful			

No. 8

City in Japan
Travelled by horse
Person subject to an attack
Soothing remedy
Edible nut
Andre ___: tennis player
Relations
A perfumed liquid (3,2,7)
Not mapped
Trees of the genus Ulmus
Small berrylike fruit
Work spirit
Went down on one knee
Business degree (abbr)
Large bag
Russian fighter aircraft
Device that makes electricity
'Be quiet!'
___ Efron: US actor
Erase
Peter Pan character
Sooty's girlfriend
Saw (anag)
Person gliding on ice
Recording medium
Lubricates
Annoy
Popular beverage
Performed on stage
The sound of a dove
Finding ___: 2003 film
Parent / teacher group (inits)
Part of a curve
Metal container; is able to
Soft touch
Bravo
Encounter; come across
Remove; excise
Blind salamander
Large body of water
Boyfriend or male admirer
Locale of a famous leaning tower
Eccentric
Pulls along forcefully
Tool similar to an axe
Totals
Texter's digression (inits)
Garment with straps
Rapper from New York
By now
Speak without preparation (2-3)
Discuss an idea casually
Study the night sky
Future flower
George Bernard ___: Irish playwright
Valuable thing

No. 9

Umberto ___: author		Suitability	Residue from a fire		___ Blyton: writer		Spain and Portugal	Throat of a voracious animal	Spiny cactus fruit (7,4)	River in Germany	Cereal grass
James ___: US actor					Car part						
							Military force				
Deposit (anag)	Advanced degree (2,1)				___ Redding: US singer		Sage				
Holier than ___: phrase	Brick carriers		Person who exploits others	Uncouth person (informal)				African antelope		___ de Cologne: perfume	People in jail
				19th Greek letter				___ Nishikori: Japanese tennis star			
Wife of Saturn				Jewel		Bob ___: US singer					
Sediment						___ Hathaway: actress		Tasty (informal)			
Forefather					Assist		Things that may happen	Hard rock		Company with under 500 staff (inits)	
Tenth month (abbr)	Black Sea peninsula		Clear or obvious								
			Quick meal	Catch fire							
Des ___: desirable house (informal)				Wishes for							
Pubs					Computer core (inits)	Umpire (abbr)	Wedding words (1,2)		BBC rival (inits)	Stimulus	Become firm
___ culpa				Reviewers							
Fled from captivity								Day after Mon. (abbr)			
Enquire				Flying saucer (inits)				Animal doctor			

No. 10

- Barack ___: former US President
- Word that identifies a thing
- Think logically
- Movable barrier
- Ben-___: epic film
- Fit for cultivation (of land)
- Lowest order of chivalry (inits)
- Maker
- Variety of peach
- Style of popular dance music
- Moby-Dick captain
- Increment
- Lists of restaurants dishes
- Long period of time
- Cocktail
- ___ off: fall asleep
- Power over others
- Obesity scale (inits)
- ___-Man: classic arcade game
- Third Gospel
- Be aware of
- ___ Vegas: city in Nevada
- Research place (abbr)
- Strong gusts of wind
- ___ Horne: actress and singer
- Used to be
- Website address (inits)
- Cheek (slang)
- Beeping device
- Small amount of something
- Ceases
- South Korean car maker
- Bambi's aunt
- Small numbered cube
- Annoy constantly
- ___ Arbor: city in Michigan
- Perfect scores
- Colourless gas with formula C_2H_6
- Auction offer
- The gist of the matter
- Caribbean country
- Venerable ___: English monk
- Vineyard (in France)
- High lending practice
- Not clothed or covered
- Coalition of countries
- ___ Leppard: rock band
- Stream of liquid
- Pad (anag)
- Swedish airline
- Let air escape from a valve
- Peephole in a door; traitor
- Light brown cane sugar
- ___ Paulo: city in Brazil
- Musical staff sign
- Sorts

No. 11

Farm vehicle	Act of moving around an axis	Battery size	Roof flue		Workroom of a painter		Limb	Standard		Shola ___: singer	Divisions of companies
							Towards the stern	Boy			
Honolulu's island					Title used for a French woman						
					Large black dung beetle	Jamaican style of music		Empty space between two objects			
Of sedate character		In the middle of						Film ___: gritty film genre	'Goodness me!' online (inits)	Note of debt (inits)	
Alcoholic beverage		Cranny					What a spider weaves				
				Uncooked (of meat)				Annual car test (inits)			
Double helix molecule		Concurring		Make beer or ale	One circuit of a track	Open to suggestion		Sticky substance			
			Reveal indiscreetly					Fourth Gospel	Weigh down	What did you say?	
Interdict	___ Winehouse: singer		Roughly force into place				Organ of sight				
			Fencing sword					Place			
Sound of a cat					Insect larvae						
			Woman's first public appearance (informal)	Abu Dhabi's location (inits)				Type of dagger		___ Oyu: mountain	Amartya ___: Indian economist
Farewell remark	They often have photos (abbr) (1,2)				Secret agent		Parts of mins.				
Popular sport	Country in the Himalayas						Arthur ___: former US tennis player				
					Thomas ___: American inventor						

No. 12

Electronic security device (7,5)		Large web-footed bird	Casual but stylish (of clothing)	Island where Napoleon was exiled	Bind	Upper part of the body		Swagger		Least expensive	Horse colour
Surprise result						Town in Surrey					
Reproduce										Type of tooth	
Spherical body						Stage play					
Former Italian currency					Upright pillars		On top of				
Statute				Inn							Bewildered
Light beams					Peter Pan character		State of confusion; disorder	Unhappy			
			Dashboard letters (inits)	Large island of Indonesia							
Cooling tool		Back up		French lady (abbr)				Area of a church	Affirmative vote	Enclosure for sheep (in Scotland)	
Viper				Entrap							
Strong drink				Trialled or tested							
			Former partners	Not at home	Mountain pass	Grasp	Shape formed by flying geese				Highest point
Unit of current	Soft juicy fruit						Pigment; stain		___ Cantrell: US R&B singer	Musical instrument (abbr)	
Evergreen tree								Degree in a science subject (abbr) (1,2)			
Full of nerve	Actually							Hit hard			
					Top quality						

No. 13

Striped animal	Feeling of boredom	Halloween shout	Line; argument		Roll of bank notes		Bartender in The Simpsons	Fruits with pips	Tithes (anag)		Internet connection device
					Public speaker						
Pasta strip							Advanced degree (2,1)				Tolled
At this moment				Girl group who sang Waterfalls	Inspires fear and wonder	Eg from Tokyo	Look closely; squint				
Tsunamis (5,5)		Naps	___ Mahal: mausoleum at Agra				Capital of Peru				
										Consent to	
___ Doyle: character in Frasier	Spheres		Edible mushroom				Adult male deer				
			Allot justice	Used a chair				Clothing	Letters of a language		Big ___: London sight
US rock band (inits)				Breathe	Vessel or duct		The reigning king				
								Sheltered side			
Person who sees something		Make fun of someone						Writing instrument			
Short cylindrical piece of wood	Release; give out	County in SE England						Tibetan Buddhist monk		Not stereo	Small social insects
			Joke		___ up on: find out about	Eg Oxfam (inits)	Game emulating an activity (informal)				
Speaks ill of								___ Jovi: US rock band			
			Army unit								
Light boat adapted for rowing		Snake toxin						Lean-___: simple shelters			

No. 14

Pay tribute to another
Low protective wall
Vestiges
Great Lake of North America
___ Brown: US author
Skewer
Turf out
Foretells
Prying; overly curious

Made a choice
Evita's surname

Account of events
Work spirit

Small particle
Edits (anag)

Speed contest
Eg hydrogen or carbon
Large town

Imitate
Clasp
A thing that measures

Check; exam
Furniture retailer
A person's head
___ Cruise: actor

Possible URL ending
Dead end

Place
Carry on
Olive-green mountain parrot
Woes
___ Maria: liqueur
___ Luthor: Superman villain

Fourth month (abbr)
Ennoble

A sheep in its second year
Workshop or studio

Tardy
Parched
Small piece of something
Parts of mins.
Negligent
Jekyll's alter ego

For each
Thick slices
'Be quiet!'
US crime fighters (inits)
Flee

Journals
Cook in hot oil

Satisfied a desire
Sew
Flower that is not yet open

Holy place

No. 15

Keep away from	Go quickly (archaic)	Taciturn		Develop	Becomes less severe	Many times (literary)		Hot volcanic rock		Female relative	Stealthy
				Bottle top		Old French currency					
Vary the pitch of the voice								___ Kilmer: famous actor			
						Chair	Eric ___: Hulk actor				
Pull back from	Least young							Rotate	Wet thoroughly	Silvery fish of the carp family	
Very powerful arms (inits)				Opposite of old				___ James: actor			
Gurgling sound	___ Flynn Boyle: actress		Pain or discomfort (informal)	___ chi				Lyric poem			
				Marks of a zebra							
Whichever				Joke	___ Koussi: mountain in Chad	Roald ___: author		___ Gadot: Israeli actress	___ Green: French actress	Decay	
Torn (of clothes)							One of the Spice Girls				
			___ Thurman: Hollywood star				River in England				
Hoover (abbr)	Wipe out										
Airships	Was in first place		___ tai: light rum cocktail	Adobe file format	Type of baleen whale		Jamaican style of music	Head covering	Gun	Also	Male offspring
						Closes					
Avoid						Musical toy					
Apotheosis											

No. 16

Raised floor or platform
Ballroom dance
___ Dhabi: part of the UAE
Revolver (informal)
Unit of time (abbr)
Code signal of distress (inits)
Doing nothing
Juicy citrus fruit
Make less sharp

Songbird

Calculating machine
___ Hill: US R&B group
Condemn to destruction

Eg pecan
Came across
Sudden misfortune
Secondary personality (5,3)
Solid ground

Very convincing
Doctor
Business degree (abbr)
After the beginning of

Happen again

Item of furniture one sleeps on
Engrave; carve
Very small child
Microbe

Brass instrument
Marry
Spice made from nutmeg
Relating to education and scholarship
Fantastical creature

Blue ___: bird
Predatory fish
Sin (anag)
___ & Stimpy: US animated sitcom

___-de-sac: dead end

Dweller
Spree
Dog's bark

Farewell remark
Sweet potatoes
Crime of burning something
Art ___: design style
Roman censor
Large antelope

River in Germany
Loud noise
Large deer
___ Kapital: Karl Marx work

Changed or modified
Make imperfect

Exuberant merriment

Text message (inits)
Positions in a hierarchy
Brian ___: English physicist

No. 17

Religious sacrament	An opening	Tavern; bar	Farm vehicle		Seaport in N Spain		I wonder...	Lids (anag)		First woman	Obvious (4-7)
							Lubricate	___ Dennis: TV presenter			
Type of knitting stitch					Reason for doing something						
					Short profile of someone (informal)	___ Ramsey: football manager		___ Amitri: Scottish band			
Skewered meat		Inner circle						Brazilian soccer legend	Tree	Zodiac sign	
Currency of Belgium		Work hard					Wonderful (informal)				
				Not on				Monetary unit of Bulgaria			
Beer container		Cold Spanish tomato soup		Protruding part of the lower jaw	Mock	Language used by an individual		Me (humorous)			
			Child's bed					Deceptive manoeuvre	Candid	Type of dagger	
Sound of snoring	___ Saldana: US actress		Removed from sight				Replace				
			Large wading bird					Criticise strongly			
Unwrap a present					Set of clothes						
			Wander aimlessly	Vestment worn by clergy				Varnish resin		Snow runner	Pouch; enclosed space
___ Arthur: US actress	Computer graphics (inits)				Climbing vine		Be at a ___: be puzzled				
Sullen; morose	Total disorder						Paul ___: singer				
					Plan						

No. 18

Snappy animal, for short	Drowned river valley	Extremely rarely (4,2,1,4,4)		Division of a group	Position in rugby (3,4)	Deranged		The leg below the ankle		Lipid	Gymnastic devices
				Towards the stern		High up					
Breathed in								Blade for rowing a boat			
						Live (anag)	___ James: US singer				
Appease	Book of the Bible							Loosen up	Type of vase	Pronoun used to refer to a ship	
Not bright; darken				___ Maria: prayer				Unique product feature (inits)			
Celestial body	Country in western Africa		___ de Janeiro: Brazilian city	___' Kim: US rapper				17th Greek letter			
				Soft woven fabric							
Broad sash				Used to be	Female sheep	Tear apart		Old Testament priest	Mauna ___: Hawaiian volcano	Pointed tool	
Scowl							Vivacity				
			Wonder				Rob ___: actor in The West Wing				
Thee	Must haves										
Breed of dog	Bravo		Internet access method (inits)	Piece of pasture	Make a mistake		Metric unit equal to 100 square metres	Roughly force into place	Miner's find	Adult males	Creative activity
						Smell					
Opposite of a winner						Less common					
Expansion											

No. 19

Japanese noodle	Person who finds something	At hand when needed (2,3)		Bring on oneself	Lived (anag)	Novel by Vladimir Nabokov	Steal livestock		___ Air: area of Los Angeles		Type of triangle
				Challenge					Stubborn		Break suddenly
Unwilling to believe											
Disco ___: The Simpsons character				Vessel or duct				Container for rubbish			
___ B: US rapper						Nikola ___: inventor and physicist					
			Dulls	Ha ha online (inits)				Touch gently			
Surpass		List of food options		Not any of	___ Green: French actress	Depart from					Of a bishop or bishops
US rapper							Join together as one	Born			
Take away							Freshwater fish				
Entrap								___ chi			
			Global trade group (inits)		Gaze fixedly		Lean-___: simple shelters	Ernie ___: South African golfer			
___ Hill: US R&B group	___ Rida: US rapper	Island of the Inner Hebrides		Hardens					Oil cartel (inits)	Robert De ___: Taxi Driver actor	
Healthy				Lie		Possessed		Yoko ___: Japanese artist			
Washing sponges								Seed of an apple			
			___ Gershwin: lyricist				Wife of Zeus				
___ Howard: US film director	Ratio of reflected to incident light							Mountain pass			

No. 20

Dry red wine	___ Hayes: US singer	Blind salamander	Handsome crow		Touch gently		Performed an action	Duplicity	Line on a weather map		Piece of code to automate a task
					Eg from New Delhi						
Scolded strongly							Computer key				Prod (anag)
___ Winehouse: singer				Navigation aid (abbr)	US state	Branch of geometry	Thin rope				
Fear of heights		Relating to country life	Obtained				Seal of the Archbishop of York				
										First Greek letter	
Canine warning sound	Building covering		Drink a little				Snare				
			Strong criticism	Gosh!				Guessing game for children (1,3)	Pennant		Japanese monetary unit
Clumsy person				Form a mental picture	Fasten together		Edgar Allan ___: US writer				
								Definite article			
Sweet on a stick		Friend (Spanish)						Hurried			
Solemn pledge	Word said on making a mistake	___ West: US rapper						Catherine ___: a wife of Henry VIII		Justin ___: golfer	___ Geller: Friends character
			Dry and mocking		Eleventh month (abbr)	Consumed food	___ Goodman: dance judge				
A number defining position								Sound of a cow			
			Toneless (anag)								
Secret agent		Number of deadly sins						Des ___: desirable house (informal)			

No. 21

Affirm with confidence	Mammal that feeds on blood (7,3)	Electronic message		Moved slowly	Enemy	High ball in tennis	Refined in manner		Pasture		Extremely impressive
				Smoke passage					Lateness		___ Penn: actor
Makes better											
Atlas page				Decline				Playing card			
Spike used by a climber						Main artery					
			Zest; liveliness	Horse shade				___ Brown: US author			
Nothing		Narrow road		Test (anag)	___ David: US lyricist	___ Clapton: English guitarist					Normally
___ Cuthbert: actress							___ acid: protein building block	Eg pecan			
Small chicken							Depend upon				
Cherubic								Plant liquid			
			Cheek (slang)		Skirmish		Female pronoun	___ Lanka: island country			
Pickup vehicle in Australia	Expert; master	Plant used for flavouring		Kate ___: English model					Release; give out	Close by	
21st Greek letter				The opposite of downs		Used a chair		Aunt ___: Bambi character			
Drive back by force								___ Gibson: US actor			
			Legume				Clock face				
Expression of surprise (informal)	Attacks on all sides							Attempt to do			

No. 22

Plant storage organs

Part of a sleeve

Simple; unrefined

Empty space

Fluffy scarf

Hostility

Farewell remark

Antique; not modern (3-9)

Delaying

Troubles in mind or body

Comply with an order

Female opera singers

Suit

Water barrier

Painting medium

___ Tyler: US actress

Worthless

BBC rival (inits)

Summer time setting (inits)

Capture a piece in chess

Examine quickly

Popular beverage

___ Burton: US film director

Centre

Thin narrow piece of wood

Workout sites

___ DiFranco: US singer

Our star

Makhaya ___: South African cricketer

Tavern; bar

Bite at persistently

Young goat

Allow

Fastener

___ MacGraw: Love Story star

Pot

Fight off

Substance present in cereal grains

Bleat of a sheep

Fruit of a rose

Unit of type-size

Word that identifies a thing

Game emulating an activity (informal)

Repasts

Stringed instrument

Splendid display

Nay (anag)

___ Lipa: English singer

Touch gently

Adult males

Chocolate powder

Piece of information

Have a wavy motion

Hit hard

Small horse

Trembling poplar

No. 23

Strong thick rope	Plentiful	Young male	Illumination unit		Stream of liquid		Fairy (literary)	South African antelope	Look out		Fills up
					Safety device in a road vehicle						
Garrulous; insolent							___ up: agitated				Exchange for money
Eucharist container				Solemn promise	___ Rickman: English actor	Genteel and feminine in manner	Female sheep (pl)				
Device for making coffee		Detection technology	___ Kilmer: famous actor				Support or foundation				
										___ Dushku: US actress	
Deranged	Help to commit a crime		Roll of bank notes				Ship's backbone				
			Run at a moderate pace	Greek goddess of the night				Long poem	Innkeeper		El ___: Spanish hero
Wooden item used in cricket				Form of an element	Cooling tool		Road vehicle				
								Gun			
Fantastic		City in Japan						Of a low standard			
___ Hanks: US actor	Sore (anag)	Printer powder						Nervous twitches		Particles around a comet	Crush with a sharp blow
			Blend together		___ Francisco: city in California	Explosive substance	Greek goddess of the dawn				
Retaliatory action								Domestic bovine animal			
			All-round view								
___ Luthor: Superman villain		Openings for air; outlets						___ King Cole: US jazz pianist			

No. 24

Parent / teacher group (inits)
Not well (5,3,7)
19th Greek letter
Stock of money
Building for gambling
Consumed food
Measure of heat
Deciduous tree
Wily
Skirt worn by ballerinas
Lessens
Narrate
Yellow fruits
Thing that fails to work properly
Arthur ___: a Wimbledon champion
TV award
Benicio del ___: actor
Curse; solemn promise
___ Sharif: Egyptian actor
Small social insect
Pulls a vehicle
Opposite of no
These remove pencil marks
Sooty's girlfriend
Organ of sight
Cash dispenser (inits)
Boolean operator
Electrician
Historic nobleman
Suggestive
__/_ whole: in general (2,1)
Brave person; idol
Computer key
Wet thoroughly
Soar; rush
Des ___: desirable house (informal)
Abu Dhabi's location (inits)
Classify
Restore confidence to
Snug and nice to wear
Cleaning item
Pouch; enclosed space
Evergreen conifer
Halt
Tap (anag)
___ Ferdinand: footballer
Extremity
Annoy constantly
First woman
Secret retreat
Unit of resistance
Cleaned its feathers (of a bird)
Desist from
___ Maria: prayer
Attempt to do
On one's ___: alone
___ up on: find out about

No. 25

Large grocery stores		Need	Grime or dirt	Give out	Fist bump	___ Stewart: ex-England cricketer		Make law		Viewers	Dote (anag)
Spurred on						Smallest quantity					
Everlasting										Capital of Vietnam	
Furnish or supply						Secret store					
Smallest pig of the litter					Horizontal supporting beams		Country bordered by Libya and Sudan				
Russian fighter aircraft				Young cat							Smudges
Extent of a surface					___ Major: the Great Bear		Flightless birds	Steal			
			Shrill bark	Domestic implement							
Dr ___: US record producer		Rayon fabric		US rock band (inits)				Letters and parcels generally	Rubbish container	Deer	
One of the Gabors				Sleep							
Turn upside down				Attacks							
			Regretted	Look at amorously	Pronoun used to refer to a ship	Dispatched	Fountain pen contents				Back of the neck
Donkey	Annoyed						Born		High mountain	Trouble in mind or body	
Harden								Battery size			
Type of leather	Moon goddess in Greek mythology							Cheek (slang)			
					Building devoted to worship						

No. 26

Receptacle for cigarette residue	Dropping a catch (in ball games)	Magic spell	Quiver		Robinson ___: novel		Affirmative vote	A group of three		South African political party (inits)	Celebrity
							In the capacity of (formal)	Knock vigorously			
South American country					Relating to horses						
					Kind of flat hat	What did you say?		Text scanning process (inits)			
Repairs		Variety of coffee						Open-air swimming pool	Opposite of outs	Expected at a certain time	
Female child		Boyfriend or male admirer					Excavate				
				Advanced degree (2,1)				Religious sister			
Soviet security police (inits)		Having dark hair		Bargain event	Me (humorous)	Partially hidden		Large salt water body			
			Type of air pollution					Calf-length skirt	Act of entering	Excavated soil	
Computer core (inits)	___ Grier: US actress		Final line on an agenda (inits)				Be nosy				
			Slip (anag)					Eg almond or pecan			
___ Hathaway: actress					Rough and uneven (of a cliff)						
			Bristle-like appendage	Purchase				___ Joly: English comedian		___ Rida: American rapper	Heavy weight
French lady (abbr)	Keyboard key				Small piece of something		Neatly skilful; agile				
Perfume	Two times						Capital of Norway				
					Small oval plum						

No. 27

Camera image (abbr)		Let it stand		Eg Sir and Dame		Speed relative to sound		Language closely related to Thai	Alumnus of a public school (3,3)		___ Air: area of Los Angeles
Nationally		Device for catching rodents		Sodium chloride		___ vera: used in cosmetics					Shows tiredness
Sum; add up						Trough for carrying bricks				Fine-tuned	
			Sheltered side				Keenness	Texter's digression (inits)			
Former French coin	Raps (anag)		Russian monarch					Possess			
Become firm				Unsteady gait	Small body of water		Sight organs				
Letters at the end of page one (inits)				Small green vegetable				Home	___ Lanka: island country		Chopped
What painters create				Sphere or globe				Jamaican style of music			
				Yoko ___: Japanese artist				The reigning king			
Scamp	Removed the skin							Silvery fish of the carp family			
Annoy		Bond movie (2,2)		Norse god of thunder	Amartya ___: Indian economist				Horse sound	Catherine ___ Jones: Welsh actress	
			Capital of the Ukraine		Recede		Long and narrow inlet		Stamped letter enclosure (inits)		___ Beatty: US actor
Shallow recess						Ascended					
			Morally compel								
___ Saldana: US actress	Action word					In front					

No. 28

Perhaps
First Greek letter
Not me
Flower that is not yet open
Writing instrument
Cereal plant
Stadiums
Far away
Not in good physical condition
Hankers after
Living room
Umpire (abbr)
Paper quantity
Dessert (informal)
Lie
Song for a solo voice
Be envious of
Rime (anag)
Mammal that feeds on blood (7,3)
Lesser
Wonderful (informal)
Write down
Consent to
Small truck
Throb
Large
Clothing line
Short pins that taper at one end
Dog's bark
Hearing organs
Food of the gods
Introverted
Police officer
___ Portman: actress
Belonging to us
Evergreen coniferous tree
Not inspiring; apathetic (informal)
A lament
Measuring instrument
Ottoman governor
Statute
Pal
Spread by scattering
Jumps on one foot
Opposite of fail
Pace
Label
Very powerful arms (inits)
Friend (French)
Tasty (informal)
Corridor
Used a chair
Vaccinate
Staleness of air in a room
Darken
Type of viper

No. 29

Sound reflection	Make amends for	Moist (of air)		Loves uncritically	Speak; total	Type of dagger	Coop up		Eccentric; strange		Goodwill
				Sued (anag)					State of separation		Departs
Amazingly good											
French lady (abbr)				Involuntary spasm				Way to up website views (inits)			
Ski run						Opposite of below					
			___ Armstrong: US astronaut	Floor mat				___ Angeles: city in California			
___ Danson: US actor		Journey		Route	Eg Cambridge or LSE (informal)	Israeli airline (2,2)					Inhabitant of our planet
Increase in intensity (4,2)							Animal that eats bamboo	Golf peg			
___ Grande: US singer							___ Turner: US singer				
Leaning at an angle								Text scanning process (inits)			
			And so on (abbr)		Annoy		___ Vegas: city in Nevada	Tennis court divider			
Seller (informal)	State of matter	River in central Russia		Dark cloud of smoke					Among	Othello villain	
Stomach				Pig		Sprinted		Be ill			
The ___: radio soap opera								___ tai: light rum cocktail			
			Egg cells				Indication				
Type of savings account (abbr)	I Am ___: film starring Will Smith							Canine			

No. 30

State of being in disrepair
Ask for; try to obtain
Linger aimlessly
Seek (anag)
Brownish yellow
Complain bitterly
Leaves out
Lists
Roster
Small body of land
Up and about
Spitting image
Inactive
Horror film directed by Ridley Scott
Threshold
Large holes in the ground
Phoenician warship
___ colada: cocktail
Frozen water
Fish with thick lips
Large waterbirds
Dreadful
Jelly or culture medium
Bluish green colour; duck
Unit of energy
Pitcher
A dancer or singer
Floor covering
Citrus fruits
Command to a horse
Clock face
Expression of alarm
Rays that can damage skin (abbr)
Note of debt (inits)
Wolfgang ___ Mozart: composer
Possible URL ending
Release someone from duty
Pubs
Gala
Hill
Chinese monetary unit
Alias initials
Mountain system in Europe
Once __/__ blue moon (2,1)
Attractively stylish
Secret agent
Young dog
Tree
Having solidified from lava (of rock)
Friend
___ Way: famous Roman road
Catch or snare
Unique product feature (inits)
Insect larvae

No. 31

- Doglike mammal
- Cried
- Magician in Arthurian legend
- Italian wine region
- Diving bird
- European country
- ___-haw: donkey sound
- Erase trumpet (anag)
- Universe as a whole
- Simplicity
- Wise man
- Impudent; full of spirit
- Pertaining to birth
- ___ Turner: US musician
- Deserving affection
- Australian singer and songwriter
- Eject diva (anag)
- Ernie ___: South African golfer
- ___-Man: classic arcade game
- Extinct bird
- Finishes
- Variety of lettuce
- Windows precursor
- Body of running water
- Check; exam
- Impose a tax
- Tenth month (abbr)
- ___ Aviv: city in Israel
- Parasitic insect
- Sound of relief
- Stitches
- Large black dung beetle
- Umberto ___: author
- Stomach muscles (informal)
- Disco ___: The Simpsons character
- Type of beer
- Facial feature
- Praying ___: insect
- Chop or cut
- Cooking appliance
- Settee
- Concave roof
- Relax; do nothing (informal)
- High renown
- Lead singer of U2
- Coalition of countries
- UK air force (abbr)
- ___ Kapital: Karl Marx work
- ___ Bon Jovi: US singer
- ___ James: actor
- Surface upon which one walks
- Martial arts schools
- Type of pasta
- ___ Paulo: city in Brazil
- Cook
- Church council

No. 32

Declare to be the case	Coerces into doing something	Note down	Expressed audibly		Stick to		Big ___: London sight	Revolve around quickly		Ab ___: from the very beginning	Resound
							Help	___ favor: please (Spanish)			
Philip ___: US novelist					Local inhabitant						
					Uncooked (of meat)	Old Testament priest		Eleventh month (abbr)			
Type of coffee drink		Made a mistake						Niels ___: Danish physicist	Olive ___: Popeye character	Chris ___: British cyclist	
Make a hole by drilling		True and actual					Tasteless items (informal)				
				Humour; funniness				Rude youth (informal)			
Type of computer port (inits)		Eg rugby or tennis (4,4)		Asian cuisine	Eighth month (abbr)	Shape of the waxing moon		Strong alkaline solution			
			Discretion					Former Italian currency	Freezing (3-4)	Flee	
Cohere	___ de Cologne: perfume		Ben-___: epic film				___ Lynam: TV presenter				
			Matured					Snip			
Jai ___: game like pelota					Tranquil						
			One of the Seven Dwarfs	Copies into an email (abbr)				Disallow		President Lincoln (for short)	___ Mendes: film director
Cuddle	Increase in amount				'Well that was silly!'		Fluffy scarves				
Large tree	Lament						Jessica ___: actress				
					Type of bicycle						

No. 33

Stroll	Civilian dress	Male sibling (informal)	Negligent		Wetland		Used to be	Black Sea peninsula	Pester		Heavy noble gas
					Bow and arrow expert						
Seventh planet							Moved quickly on foot				Tennis court dividers
Mammal with a bushy tail				Title of a married woman	Once more	Horse of light tan colour	Type of golf club				
Sleeps through winter		Tribe (anag)	Atlas page				Long flowing hair				
										Nairobi is the capital here	
Revolver (informal)	___ Sandler: comedian		French for 'salt'				Requests				
			Sleeveless cloak; headland	Expression of admiration				Rubbish containers	Everlasting		Cutting tool
Ant and ___: presenting duo				Skill	Craze		At this moment				
								US R&B musician			
Flammable liquid		Musical instrument						Throat of a voracious animal			
Place where one sees animals	Still to be paid	Equip						Soft creamy cheese		Small quantity	Saw; observed
			Clumsy person		That man	Sprite	Place				
Fighting vessel								Plaything			
			Imitate								
___ Leppard: rock band		Well cared for						Boy			

No. 34

Very masculine		Useful implement		Mineral of lead sulphide		Pleased		Web access company (inits)	Long-billed wading birds		Stamped letter enclosure (inits)
Teacher		Herald		Patron saint of Norway		___ Kudrow: Friends actress					Verse
___ Berry: actress						Printer resolution (inits)				Illness	
			Small social insect				Fruit-filled pastries	Put down			
In favour of	Long walk		Mythical man-goat creature					___ Burton: US film director			
That man's				Swords	___ Stravinsky: Russian composer		Small island				
__/_ bad way: unwell (2,1)				Outs opposite				Propose; utter	Made-up statement		A single time
Soviet security police (inits)				Obtained				Zodiac sign			
				Egg cells				Public house			
Change course	Rue doing something							And so on (abbr)			
___ Tyler: US actress		The south of France		People in general	Seller (informal)				Ways or tracks	Dell	
			Action word		Thee		Health resort		Decay		Apiece
Lure an animal into a trap						Parts (anag)					
			Legal ambiguity								
Coniferous tree	Capital of Azerbaijan					Daisy-like flower					

No. 35

Exemption from a rule		A thousand thousand	Grown-ups	Precious stones	Bravo	Holed a putt		Long wooden seat		Bleak; stark	Japanese beverage
Insect stage						Assists in a crime					
Tennis court boundaries										God of love	
Long cloud of smoke						Bump					
Sell (anag)					Break rules		Hint				
Louse egg				Accident							Manages
Neither good nor bad (2-2)					Pulled apart		Ready to eat (of fruit)	Involuntary spasm			
			Musical ability	Submarine weapon							
___ Solo: Star Wars character		Loud and hoarse		___-Wan Kenobi: Star Wars character				Bone of the forearm	Pasture	Home for a pig	
___ Gershwin: lyricist				Drive back by force							
Blade for rowing a boat				Small holes in cloth or leather							
			Capital of Italy	In a lazy way	Garment with straps	Not sweet	Negative vote				Left side of a ship
Antelope	Babies' beds						Global trade group (inits)		Flightless bird	State of matter	
___ Wilson: 28th US President								Sense of oneself			
___ Affleck: US actor	Diacritical mark of two dots							Spoil			
					Vigorous; strong and healthy						

No. 36

- Small woodland
- Earthy pigment
- Edgar Allan ___: US writer
- Plant of the pea family
- Monetary unit of Albania
- Father
- Classify
- Art of growing dwarfed trees
- Last
- Language
- Baked
- Male offspring
- Departs
- ___ Jude: Beatles song
- Zig and ___: puppet duo
- Moby-Dick captain
- In a disorderly manner (4-4)
- Obstacle
- Triangular pyramids
- Medicine
- Hit forcibly
- Capital of Norway
- Latin American dance
- Day before Tuesday (abbr)
- Follow orders
- ___ Gadot: Israeli actress
- Nervous twitches
- Soak (anag)
- Type of sandwich (inits)
- Emaciated
- At work (2-3-3)
- Over there (literary)
- Short profile of someone (informal)
- Despicable person
- ___ West: US actress
- Indian dish with lentils
- Eg Oxfam (inits)
- Made still
- Australian arboreal marsupial
- Light brown colour
- Wild ox
- Having inherent ability
- Increase in size
- Chest muscles, briefly
- Closing section of music
- Pace
- Item that unlocks a door
- ___ Thumb: folklore character
- Vineyard (in France)
- Female pronoun
- Charm; enchant
- Note down
- Portend
- Layer of a folded material
- Thigh bone
- Bread roll

No. 37

Christmas show (abbr)
Cajole
Symbolic
School bedroom (abbr)
Level golf score
Utterly senseless
Unwell

Adverse
Disciples
Document allowing entry to a country
Quartz-like gem
Chris ___: British radio DJ

A poison
Title of a married woman
Insanity

A knight
Happening repeatedly
___ Thurman: actress

Basic monetary unit of Peru
Created
Case (anag)
Sprinted

Large extinct flightless bird
Lanes
Blast of a horn
Totals

Tool for making holes in leather
Stomach (informal)
Molten rock
___ Beatty: US actor
Chooses

___ Amitri: Scottish band
Rita ___: British singer
The Matrix role

Possible URL ending
Psychic ability (inits)

Small pond
A complex whole
Summer time setting (inits)

River bottom
Breed of domestic ox
Police officers (informal)
Short sleep
Musical instrument with keys
Tracey ___: English artist

Haul
Pad (anag)
Roll of bank notes
Propel a boat
Utter

Fret about
Heats up

Baseless distrust of others

___ Lipa: English singer
Struggle for air
Fluffy and soft

No. 38

Decorated a cake	Thick and heavy shoe	Long-___ owl: bird		Draw or bring out	Board game	Fix the result in advance	Waterproof jacket		'Goodness me!' online (inits)		Freed
				Steve ___: British ex-athlete					Country in Central America		Completely fill
Nitrous oxide (8,3)											
Monstrous humanoid creature				Sense of oneself				___ Stubbs: English actress			
Actions						Respond to					
			Lead singer of U2	Australian singer and songwriter				Bind			
Advanced degree (2,1)		Showing vigour or spirit		___ colada: cocktail	Brian ___: Roxy Music musician	Retain					Boat
Push forward							West Indian dance	Type of computer (abbr)			
Type of sandwich							Statistics and facts				
Efficiency								Allow			
			Cease		School of fish		Healthcare provider (inits)	Novel by Vladimir Nabokov			
Shed tears	Fruit preserve	Military unit		Tune					Subject to debate	The Christmas festival	
First month (abbr)				Website address (inits)		Flying saucer (inits)		US R&B musician			
Laborious								Belonging to us			
			UK air force (abbr)				Run ___ Run: 1998 thriller film				
I wonder...	Colour of a lemon							Five plus five			

No. 39

Feline		Involving space and time (4-11)	Fourth month (abbr)		Motivate; desire to act		Walk stealthily	Health resort	Clay pottery	Ignited	Small winged insect
From a distance					Reflexive pronoun						
							Bucket				
Temporary measure	Midge ___: Ultravox musician				Listen to		Tray (anag)				
Repeat an action	Time periods		Woodwind instrument	Pig				Pleased		One (Spanish)	Flat slabs
				Slippery fish				Small shelter			
Mock				Guitar with four strings (abbr)		Sporting stadium					
Lover or love affair						Spots		Person of wealth (informal)			
Look for					Violate a law of God		Norwegian band (1-2)	First Pope		Loud noise	
Photo ___: publicity events	Country in Central America		Wild prank								
			Obsession	Acquire from a relative							
Goal				Tidies							
Ark builder					'Officer' order of chivalry (inits)	Expression of surprise (informal)	Terminate		Things that may happen	Food (informal)	Imitate
___ Arbor: city in Michigan				Musical wind instrument							
Receptacle for letters								Dandy			
_/__ carte: menu type (1,2)				Before in time (poetic)				Company with under 500 staff (inits)			

No. 40

Not clear	Fruit of the oak	Sticky substance	Word used to express disgust		Female chicken		Secretly email (inits)	Highly motivated	Live in		Demon
					Sacred (anag)						
Brandy							Increase the running speed of an engine				Noticed
Gosh!				Boogie; dance	Suggestion	Thieves	Egyptian goddess				
Brought into use		Robber	Baby's neckwear while eating				Disgusting				
										Large body of water	
23rd Greek letter	Leg part		Apiece				Noble gas				
			Sound of a cat	Before the present				Travelled too quickly	Highly productive		Pigment; stain
Sewn edge				Superficial wound	21st Greek letter		Item used to catch fish				
								Beam of light			
Longevity of an individual		Earthy pigment						Single in number			
Energy; bounce	Deciduous trees	Joint						Capital of Peru		Not stereo	Ship used by Jason and followers
			Genre of music		Deep anger	Fasten with stitches	___ Jude: Beatles song				
Boorish								Pro			
			Moving slowly								
Unit of current		Requiring much mastication						Sound of a dove			

No. 41

Dirt		___ Flynn Boyle: actress		Suppurate		Distort		Vessel; jolt	Makes amends for		Vineyard (in France)
Type of cloud		Reject		A single time		Partly open					Grain storage chambers
Intended						Expert; master				Make better	
			Business leader (inits)				Living things	Nothing			
Ninth month (abbr)	Lied (anag)		Makes a mistake					Style of rock music			
They prove who you are (abbr) (1,2)				Stitching	Ship's officer; friend		Cobras				
Small numbered cube				___ tai: cocktail				US state	Male aristocrat		Wild cat
Legal rule				Along with; also				Basic monetary unit of Peru			
				___ Maria: liqueur				Climbing plant			
Legendary creature	Entangle							___ & Stimpy: US animated sitcom			
26th letter		Greek cheese		Hard green gem	Cat (informal)				Estimate	Concern; worry	
			Extinct bird		School of Mahayana Buddhism		___ Farrow: US actress		Comment on a silly action		___ Harding: Welsh actor
Precious gem						Olympic award					
			Laughably small								
Did possess	Portent					Very pale					

No. 42

Third Greek letter	___ Adkins: singer	Karaoke need (informal)	Periodic publication (abbr)		Father		Pobol y ___: Welsh soap opera	Pictures	Dinner jacket		Yellow citrus fruit
					Paler						
Crown							Female parent				___ Campbell: Scream actress
Heart test (abbr)				Ballpoint pen brand	Smudge	Orange pigment found in carrots	Part of a nerve cell				
Aired		Silk dress fabric	Airer of Doctor Who (inits)				Unit of heredity				
										Ray	
___ Brown: US author	Related by blood		Mongrel dog				A few				
			Locale of a famous leaning tower	___ Doyle: character in Frasier				One's customary behaviour	At work (2-3-3)		Your (poetic)
Area of seating at Liverpool FC				Black ___: rock band	Heart of activity		Period of 24 hours				
								To the ___ degree: to the utmost			
Terminated		Vapour bath						Scotland's longest river			
Small amount of something	Sailed through	Church building						Comes together; coheres		Luxurious car (abbr)	Small Eurasian merganser
			Round bread roll		Show discontent	Lucy ___: US actress	Former measure of length				
Capable of being remedied								___ Henson: US puppeteer			
			Arduous								
___ Goodman: dance judge		Evil spirit						Knot with a double loop			

No. 43

Plant yield	Chris ___: English singer	Extremely rarely (4,2,1,4,4)		Not dense	Handbook published annually	Was in first place		Flightless bird		Bind	Science of farming
				Form of public transport		Andrew Lloyd Webber musical					
Helped to happen								Hairpiece			
						Hindu spiritual discipline	Platform leading out to sea				
Triangular bone	Pieces of writing							Eg square or circle	Computer key	Friend of Tigger	
Go quickly (archaic)				Japanese masked drama				Part of a curve			
Protective crust over a wound	Face (anag)		Short profile of someone (informal)	Heavy stove				___ Reed: US musician			
				Seat of the US Congress							
___ Titmuss: TV personality				Source of a metal	Huge mythical bird	Badger's home		Interdict	Shola ___: singer	Clothing needed for an activity	
Knocks down an opponent							Capital of Azerbaijan				
			Fish eggs				___ Khan: British boxer				
Monetary unit of Romania	Voters										
On a ship or train	Obesity scale (inits)		___ Gardner: US actress	Relieve or free from	Kapil ___: Indian cricketer		___ Vegas: city in Nevada	Large period of time	Pen point	Indian dish with lentils	Direction opposite NNW
						Gives temporarily					
Film						Operatic songs					
Unwise											

No. 44

Room attached to a house		Retorted	Imagined whilst asleep	Flat and smooth	Fishing pole	Immense		Turns over		Monarchist	Group of players
Command						Currently in progress					
Anxiously										Measuring stick	
Rapidity of movement						Coronet					
Flair					Succinct		Edible fruit				
Edge of a cup				Remains preserved in rock							Low value US coins
Animal doctors					Skin mark from a wound		The Orient	Dry (of wine)			
			Drivel; nonsense	Type of staff							
To a small extent		Fear of heights		US spy agency (inits)				Helper; assistant	Eg Cambridge or LSE (informal)	One circuit of a track	
Egg cells				Attack							
Seller (informal)				Retains (anag)							
			Spoken exam	Movable barrier	Mature	Large bodies of water	Depression				Shaft on which a wheel rotates
Port in Scotland	Roman cloaks						Take to court		Cooking utensil	Wonder	
Optical illusions								Roman goddess of peace			
Complete	Rich cake							Nocturnal bird of prey			
					Seat for two or more persons						

No. 45

- Academy award
- Minute pore in a leaf
- Body's vital life force
- Ancient boat
- Character in Despicable Me
- To some extent (informal)
- By word of mouth
- Tropical fruit
- Country in the Arabian peninsula
- Inclined
- Songbird
- Roughly force into place
- Island of the Inner Hebrides
- Uncouth person (informal)
- Female sibling (informal)
- Emotional state
- Anxious uncertainty
- Primates
- Carefully
- Strong desires
- Text message (inits)
- Long and limp (of hair)
- ___ Lewis: British singer
- Light boat adapted for rowing
- Large wading bird
- Code signal of distress (inits)
- Ivy League university
- Catch sight of
- Printer resolution (inits)
- Formal dance
- Act of retaliation
- Male person
- Insect which collects pollen
- Market a product
- Muslim festival
- ___ Amitri: Scottish band
- Aunt ___: Bambi character
- Squander money
- Forcibly open; lever
- Criticise strongly
- US crime fighters (inits)
- Gareth ___: Welsh footballer
- Mountain cry
- Prima donna
- Nave (anag)
- Helps
- Very cold
- Most hotel milk is this (inits)
- ___ Camp: Barcelona's football stadium
- Male sheep
- Report of an event
- Dagger with two sharp prongs
- 10 cubed
- Layer of a folded material
- Rise (3,2)
- ___ Dennis: TV presenter

No. 46

Propel forwards		Mineral powder		Recover		Sewing join		23rd Greek letter	Get away from		Very small
Binoculars (5,7)		Very sharp and perceptive (5-4)		Stage of twilight		Fencing sword					Move on ice
Empty spaces						Karaoke need (informal)				Cotton fabric	
			Violate a law of God				Publicly known	Heavy stove			
___ Varney: English actor	___ Moore: US actress		Intertwined segment of rope					Deep hole in the ground			
Woman's first public appearance (informal)				Made a loud and harsh sound	Compact mass		Unit of heredity				
Snake-like fish				Remove branches				Pub orders	Eg website banners (informal)		Greek god of war
US R&B musician				___ Geller: illusionist				Norwegian band (1-2)			
				Dialect of Chinese				___ es Salaam: city in Tanzania			
Rank	Tyrant							Company with under 500 staff (inits)			
Huge mythical bird		Attend (2,2)		Martial arts school	Type of computer port (inits)				Type of soup	Belonging to a woman	
			Cook		Of a low standard		The Old ___: London theatre		Distress; misery		Summer time setting (inits)
Palpitate						Promised					
			Caretakers								
Fish eggs	Nutrition					Thorax					

No. 47

Bring together into a mass

Type of respiration

Climbs

Volcano in Sicily

Sorrowful

Revolve around quickly

Marriage

Navigating

Christmas

Fertile spots in deserts

Feign (3,2)

Variety of peach

Body of rules

Expansive

Female relation

Run ___ Run: 1998 thriller film

Large monkeys

By word of mouth

'Officer' order of chivalry (inits)

Substance found in wine

Usage measuring device

Japanese food paste

Seed used in various foods

Not as much

Food (informal)

Japanese monetary unit

Large German city

Chest muscle (informal)

Matured

Weeding tool

Knocks lightly

Affirmative vote

Five plus five

Have existence

Install

Chemical element

One who assesses metals

Titled peer

Not at home

Healthcare provider (inits)

Female rabbits

Animal enclosure

Small horse

High spirits; energy

Antelope

Dry and mocking

Loud noise

___ Saldana: US actress

Technical knowledge (4-3)

Cow and yak hybrid

Chum

Pencil rubber

Charged particle

Capital of New South Wales

No. 48

Engage in argument	Container for stationery (6,4)	Hawaiian greeting		Angry	Pools (anag)	Rita ___: British singer	Character of a person		Acquire		Feeling of hatred
				Solitary					Cross or cut each other		Require
Act of explaining in detail											
Word expressing negation				Widely cultivated cereal grass				Former music magazine			
Faint bird cry						Undo					
			Rolled up tortilla sandwich	Camera type (inits)				Extremity			
___ Farrow: US actress		Sound reflection		Ride the waves	Id ___: that is to say	___ Pound: US poet					Amoral
Stopped							Triangular river mouth	Disco ___: The Simpsons character			
Level a charge against							Blood vessel				
Soon								Seb ___: British former athlete			
			Seller (informal)		___ Lewis: British singer		Two (Spanish)	Explosive substance			
The Matrix role	Novel by Vladimir Nabokov	Hit hard		Boys					Upon	___ Simone: US singer	
President Lincoln (for short)				___ Reed: US musician		Over there (literary)		___ DiFranco: US singer			
Brings to effective action								Involuntary spasm			
			Yoko ___: Japanese artist				Island of the Inner Hebrides				
Bleat of a sheep	Child who skips school							Friend			

No. 49

Game similar to bowls	Opposite one of two	River in eastern England	Cirque		26th letter		Low bank of coral	What oak trees grow from	Destroy		Extent
					Frightens; startles						
Showy and cheap							Taxi				Unable to hear
I wonder...				Large body of water	Corrosive substance	Footballers whose role is to score	Roman poet				
Shielding		Seeped	Swedish airline				Rank				
										Ascends	
Flat-topped conical hat	Eagle with a white tail		Mixture of gases we breathe				Feudal labourer				
			Slender freshwater fish	Not bright; darken				Circular storage medium	Made better		Computer graphics (inits)
Primary colour				Tell a story	___ Scala: actress and model		Fish eggs				
								___ Ryan: US actress			
Put at risk		Capital of Egypt						23rd Greek letter			
Hairpiece	Wild mountain goat	Rub out						Attend (2,2)		Fork part	Cereal grains used as food
			Gallivant		Type of computer (abbr)	__/__ rule: usually (2,1)	Timid				
Country in the West Indies								By way of			
			Capital of Uzbekistan								
___ Danson: US actor		Rot						___ Lynam: TV presenter			

No. 50

___ Pascoe: English comedian	Wipe out	Rushes		A central point	Smash into another vehicle	Chop or cut	Inborn		Father		Divisor
				Seed used in various foods					Excluding; alienating		Urge on
Going on and on (5-6)											
Born				Bristle-like appendage				Sooty's girlfriend			
Spends time doing nothing						Smell					
			Pierce with a knife	___ up: agitated				Bottle top			
Videotape letters (inits)		___ Stravinsky: Russian composer		Russian sovereign	Computer keyboard key	___ McGregor: Scottish actor					Truly
Rubbish							Christina ___: actress	Label			
Andre ___: former US tennis player							Locate or place				
Cigarette constituent								Oui's opposite			
			Computer core (inits)		English royal house		Boolean operator	Character in Despicable Me			
For each	Annoy	Freezes over		Colour lightly					Remnant	Mystique; ambience	
One given red-carpet treatment (inits)				___ Dhabi: part of the UAE		Be in debt		___ Francisco: city in California			
Republic in South America								Day after Mon. (abbr)			
			Knot with a double loop				Type of knitting stitch				
Chopping tool	Made bitter							Broad inlet of the sea			

No. 51

Camera image (abbr)		Church song		Routed (anag)		Curved shapes		Tree that bears acorns	Happy; carefree		Come together
Insistently		___ Cilmi: Australian singer		Taj Mahal's location		Loose flowing garment					Teenage years
Ballroom dance						Snow runner				Severely simple	
			Strong spirit				Improve	19th Greek letter			
Gang	Bikini parts		Extent of a surface					Small shelter			
Auction offer				Lower in value	Celestial body		Wire lattice				
Enclosure for sheep (in Scotland)				Eg use a chair				Capital of Japan	Carry a heavy object		Leg joint
Vestment worn by clergy				Also				Monetary unit of Albania			
				Ancient boat				Pot			
___ Fisher: actress	Far from the target							Command to a horse			
Decay		Crazy (informal)		Black ___: Colombian bird	On one's ___: alone				Italian cathedral	Richard ___: Hollywood actor	
			Snare		Peter ___: English comedian		Queen ___: fairy in Romeo and Juliet		Roman goddess of peace		Male teacher
Eccentric person						Sulks					
			Squid								
Indian state	Address a deity					Fighter					

No. 52

Very sad

Trucks

Frozen water spear

Ends; goals

Pad (anag)

Norse god

High lending practice

Fetch

Takes to court

Epic poem ascribed to Homer

Songs for two people

Left-wing politician

Small branch

Bend or curl

Care for; look after

Imaginary monsters

David ___: former Prime Minister

Tears open

Nothing

Solicitor

___ on: urged to do

Perceives

US space agency

Football boot grip

Compete

Home for a pig

One's savings for the future (4,3)

Variety of lettuce

Worry

What painters create

Wear away

Dandy

Ignited

Statute

Light spongy baked dish

Plaything

Human-like robot

Angers

Capital of Italy

US spy agency (inits)

Requests

Suitable

Cunning

Wetland

About

Not inspiring; apathetic (informal)

Adobe file format

Worn channel

Great courage

Expert; master

Eg taste or touch

Recreate

Top pupil in school (Scottish)

Evasive; devious

No. 53

Moisten meat	Circa	Drink a little	Very small child		Acquire; obtain		Pouch; enclosed space	Lived by	Engaging in deep thought		With a forward motion
					Fit for cultivation (of land)						
Pertaining to life							Male sibling (informal)				Transmit
Top (anag)				Ram	Chemical salt	Eg from Tokyo	Electrically charged particles				
Specified conditions		Type of chemical bond	___ Mahal: mausoleum at Agra				Chief magistrate of Venice				
										Orderly grouping	
Lair	Flightless birds		Young dog				Group of two people				
			Dominion	Floor covering				___ Wang: fashion designer	Dots indicating an omission		Bristle-like appendage
Russian space station				Eyelash cosmetic	Data transfer measure (inits)		The reigning king				
								Statute			
Long green vegetable		Slight error; oversight						___ Harding: Welsh actor			
Sharp blow	Continent	County in SE England						Omar ___: US actor		Monetary unit of Mexico	Takes an exam
			Secretly email (inits)		Frying pan	Strong alkaline solution	___ Francisco: city in California				
Writes untidily								Type of baleen whale			
			Monarchist								
Karaoke need (informal)		Rouse from sleep						Code signal of distress (inits)			

No. 54

Life force		Extremely rarely (4,2,1,4,4)	Antelope		Not new		Supplied or distributed	Dog's bark	The middle class	___ Angeles: city in California	Eek (anag)
Doesn't share					Firmly fixed						
							Eurasian crow				
Main meals	Partly digested animal food				Argues		Electrical safety device				
Turn over	Brian ___: West Indian cricketer		Bucket	US rock band (inits)				Wire lattice		Twist about a vertical axis	Imaginary
				Lyric poem				Pain or discomfort (informal)			
___ Ivanovic: tennis star				Pigment; stain		Give a solemn oath					
Attacks without warning						Big bash		Be in debt			
Skilfully; adeptly					Shape formed by flying geese		Greek letter 'N's	Organic compound		Argument against something	
___ Cantrell: US R&B singer	Rough shelter (4-2)		Fade away								
			Parasitic insect	Act of avoiding capture							
Slippery fish				Area of London (4,3)							
Run ___: go wild					Animal that oinks	Eg Cambridge or LSE (informal)	Food item from a hen		Type of savings account (abbr)	___' Kim: US rapper	Former term for euro
___ Camp: Barcelona's football stadium				Immature and childish							
Throwing a coin in the air								In such a manner; thus			
Single in number				Light boat adapted for rowing				CPU part (inits)			

No. 55

From a distance	Ahead of the times	Coral reef		Impress on paper	Indian rice dish	Ate (anag)	Burrowing long-eared mammal		Soft animal hair		Evaluation
				South American country					Suggest indirectly		Narrow strip of land
Designed for usefulness											
Heavy weight				Research place (abbr)				Former music magazine			
Favouring extreme views						Staple					
			Reduces in length	___ Geller: illusionist				Fluid used for writing			
Website address (inits)		Temporary outside shelter		Counter used in poker	Edible mushroom	___ Turner: US singer					Gullibility
Plaster for coating walls							Small antelope	Primary time standard (inits)			
Restraint							Couple				
Vapid								Foot extremity			
			___ Paulo: city in Brazil		Tycoon		Turn upside down	Cease			
Statute	Type of computer port (inits)	Plant stalk		Tiny arachnid					Breathe hard	US state	
North American nation (abbr)				Collection of paper		Epoch		___ Pot: Khmer Rouge leader			
Temporary measure								Large tuna			
			Eighth month (abbr)				An individual thing				
President Lincoln (for short)	Varied mixture of things							Plaything			

No. 56

Skilful	Distinct historical period	Involving space and time (4-11)		Increase in intensity (4,2)	Superficial area	Expression of alarm		Eminem song featuring Dido		Consume a meal	US state (5,6)
				Insect that can sting		Go in					
European deer								Sound of relief			
						On top of	After the beginning of				
Very poor person	Expressing regret							Entices	Me (humorous)	Lowest order of chivalry (inits)	
Economic stat. for a country (inits)				Character in The Simpsons				French lady (abbr)			
Mother	Paul ___: singer		Wonder	Expression of surprise (informal)				___-Wan Kenobi: Star Wars character			
				Foes							
Opposite of old				Key next to the space bar	Small numbered cube	Ride the waves		Eg website banners (informal)	Rodent	Anger	
Works dough							Song for a solo voice				
			Lucy ___: US actress				Mend with rows of stitches				
State of matter	Intrigued										
Ottawa is the capital here	Vestment worn by clergy		Gone by	Ant and ___: TV presenters	Ancient boat		Character in Despicable Me	___ Vegas: city in Nevada	Creative activity	Jack ___: comedian	Make a mistake
						A clearing in a wood					
Beer						Less common					
Film that is a great success											

No. 57

Aqualung	Island in the Bay of Naples	Guitar with four strings (abbr)	Large		Sound of a hard blow		One more than one	Endured	Japanese dress		Arboreal primate
					Ambled						
With hands on the hips							Goal				___ monster: venomous lizard
Short cylindrical piece of wood				Summer time setting (inits)	Sailed through	Foliage	Full of oneself				
___ wiper: car device		Synthetic fabric	Flexible container				___ Amos: US singer				
										Capital of Vietnam	
Nocturnal bird of prey	Blue dye		Golf ball holder				Capital of Qatar				
			Sound of a snake	Water droplets formed at night				___ Simone: US singer	Fearless and brave		As easy as ___: simple
Gosh!				Reddish marine fish	Head covering		Camera type (inits)				
								Person of wealth (informal)			
Disappears		Growl with bare teeth						Involuntary spasm			
Removed from sight	Lazy	Woodland god						Legendary creature		Fish	___ Azalea: Australian rapper
			___ Leppard: rock band		Chopping tool	Frozen water	Mud channel				
Feel very down								Breed of dog			
			Letting off								
Fantastical creature		Welcome						24-hour period			

No. 58

Aversion to change		Enlist	___ Clooney: US actor	Hubbubs	Louse egg	Beers		Town in Surrey; sheer (anag)		Plummet	Breezy
Musical instrument						___ Lewis: British singer					
State of poverty										Extra component (3-2)	
Go swiftly						Remove wool from sheep					
Makes a mistake					Pipe from which water can be drawn		Circular movement of water				
Floor mat				Composite of different species							Vascular tissue in plants
Vista					Bonus; positive		___ Sharif: Egyptian actor	Voice			
			Greek goddess of the night	Children							
Feline		Pairs		Hit hard				Pottery	Consumed food	Flee	
Very cold				Ignorant of something							
Boston Red ___: baseball team				Layer or band of rock							
			Having a sound mind	Parched	Limb used for walking	Mothers	___ & Stimpy: US animated sitcom				___ Giggs: footballer
Flightless bird	Sacred hymn or song						Bland soft food		Wild ox	___ Maria: prayer	
Sudden outburst of something (5-2)								Expression of triumph or approval			
Enclosed	Mystery; riddle							___ Gardner: US actress			
					Uttered						

No. 59

Friend (Spanish)	Lionel ___: Argentine soccer star	Family or variety	A man; fellow		Seed vessel		Owns	Eg from New Delhi	Breakfast food		Biblical tower site
					Type of living organism						
Escapes from							Crux of a matter				Wizard
Hit high into the air				Two (Spanish)	___ Musk: SpaceX founder	Essential nutrients	Hold as an opinion				
Fiendish		Greek writer of fables	___ Patel: British actor				___ Fisher: actress				
										Country in East Africa	
Belonging to him	Thought or suggestion		Drunkard				Goddess of victory in Greek mythology				
			Brass musical instrument	___ King Cole: US jazz pianist				Peel	Absolute		River blocker
Small spot				Blaze seen on November 5th	Carry a heavy object		Chicago's summer time zone (inits)				
								US R&B musician			
Type of state		Run with leaping strides						___ Grier: US actress			
Chatter	Call from a sailor	Anxiety						Diana ___: actress in The Avengers		Donated	___ Kinnear: US actor
			Knot with a double loop		School of Mahayana Buddhism	Not new	Negative vote				
On the ___: about to happen								Road vehicle			
			Eg uncle or sister								
Pull a vehicle		Girl in the Peter Pan stories						A sheep in its second year			

No. 60

State of armed conflict

Aggressive in manner

___ Koussi: mountain in Chad

Child's bed

___ Spielberg: US filmmaker

Small viper

Forged

Girl group who sang Waterfalls

Perceive

Genus of trees

Short written works

Marine flatfish

Dark red halogen

Pen point

Raised area of skin

Dark red colour

Pub rooms selling alcohol

Water, in Spain

Hernando de ___: Spanish explorer

Damp

Settlement smaller than a city

Eg bauxite

Salt lake in the Jordan valley (4,3)

Brian ___: Roxy Music musician

On one's ___: alone

Sticky substance

Sprite

In what place

Up to the time when

Short skirt

Chris ___: English singer

Moat (anag)

Strong spirit

Another word for 'Gran'

Held on to something tightly

Snow runner

Vessel

Burrowing rodent

Daughter of a sovereign

Large indefinite amount

Dissimilar

Loose white judo jackets

The small details of something

Word said on making a mistake

___ Dennis: TV presenter

Before (literary)

Internet access method (inits)

Large deer

Enclosure for sheep (in Scotland)

Violate a law of God

___ Stubbs: English actress

Account books

Rags

Garland of flowers

___ de Ré: French island

French for 'salt'

Range of knowledge

No. 61

Grows older	Expression of surprise (8,2)	Messenger		English racecourse	Cook meat in the oven	Centre of activity	Amended		___ McKellen: English actor		State of having unlimited power
				Ostrichlike bird					Method of teaching a new language		Tolkien tree creatures
Very happy (2,5,4)											
Ab ___: from the very beginning				___ Titmuss: TV personality				Dialect of Chinese			
Loves uncritically						Entice to do something					
			___ brothers: US filmmakers	Bind				Greek goddess of the dawn			
Whichever		___ Neeson: Northern Irish actor		Baby carriage	Unit of energy	Mud					Worn by the elements
Slants							Food relish	Fasten with stitches			
Long mountain chain							Plant of the grape family				
Capital of Nicaragua								Plant related to wood sorrel			
			Fourth month (abbr)		Eg Lindsey Vonn		Auction item	Item for catching fish			
Sewn edge	Norwegian band (1-2)	___ Jacobs: US fashion designer		Exchange for money					Slightly open	___ Land: 2016 film (2,2)	
Unit of current				Popular Oxford degree (inits)		Home for a pig		Beer			
Rip hats (anag)								Jolt			
			Domestic animal				Bargain event				
Bitumen	___ Baker: Bucks Fizz singer							Physics unit			

No. 62

Franz ___: novelist	Garment worn in the kitchen	Enemy	Beer container		Wooden item used in cricket		PC key	Planet	Most pleasant		Cavalry sword
					Steam rooms						
Written in verse							Mock				In a tense state
___ Varney: English actor				In what way	Horse breed	Final teenage year	Square measure				
Shameful		Evil spirit	Chinese dynasty				Require				
										Relating to sound	
Status ___: rock band	Exploits		Pallid				Remain in the same place				
			Short pins that taper at one end	Wager				Fathers	Endorsed		Ninth month (abbr)
Drink				Artistic movement (3,4)	Way to up website views (inits)		Not wet				
								___ chart: type of graph			
Set free		Germaine ___: Australian author						Fizzy drink			
Videotape letters (inits)	Pay close attention to	Rocky						Part of an egg		___ Del Rey: singer	Was aware of; understood
			Cutting tool		Tree that bears acorns	Cook in hot oil	___ Fighters: US rock band				
Become less intense (4,3)								Small truck			
			Orange plant pigment								
Long bench		Capital of Japan						Small crow			

No. 63

Rank	__/__ whole: in general (2,1)	Give in (5,2,3,5)		Scanty	Most healthy	Heart test (abbr)		Practical joke		Piece of cloth	Set a limit on (4,3,4)
				Olive-green mountain parrot		Kind of beet					
Trembling								Level golf score			
						___ Sharif: Egyptian actor	Video game company				
Victim	Public speaker							Strong cords	El ___: Spanish hero	Internet access method (inits)	
Wonder				Style of rock music				Chicago's summer time zone (inits)			
Island of the Inner Hebrides	Solemn promise		___ Winehouse: singer	Tree fluid				To some extent (informal)			
				Lever operated with the foot							
Cash dispenser (inits)				Make imperfect	Type of computer port (inits)	Goad on		Lowest order of chivalry (inits)	Charged particle	One of the Seven Dwarfs	
Lymphoid organ							The south of France				
			Small viper				Blessing				
___ Guevara: guerrilla leader	Rough air currents										
Towards a higher place	Chest muscle (informal)		Have existence	Long narrow inlet	Animal lair		___ Lanka: island country	Cooking utensil	Made-up statement	Donkey	Positive answer
						Spread out and apart (of limbs or fingers)					
Strange and mysterious						Lift up					
Freedom from dirt											

No. 64

Capital of Egypt		Having pains		Meal eaten outdoors		Michelle ___: Malaysian actress		Disco ___: The Simpsons character	Saying		River in Wales
Garments worn in bed		Grotesque figures		Heading on a list of tasks (2,2)		Catch sight of					Of definite shape
Fabric made from cellulose						Ben-___: epic film				Small beetles	
			Depression				Medical practitioner	Piercing tool			
Pro	Cloak of a priest		Where darts players throw from					Type of baleen whale			
Toothed wheel				Sculptured symbols	Related by blood		A plant grows from this				
Olive ___: Popeye character				Enquire				Light canoe	___ de Cologne: perfume		Carpe ___: seize the day
Layer of a folded material				South Korean car maker				Muslim festival			
				Very cold; slippery				___ MacGraw: Love Story star			
Profound	___ Twain: Canadian singer							Purpose			
Popular beverage		Boyfriend or male admirer		Legume	Alias initials				Female relatives	Small pond	
			Totals		Opposite of downs		Anger		Greek letter 'N's		The reigning king
Word of farewell						Interior					
			An opening								
Broken equipment	Male children					County in E England					

No. 65

Reallocate		Get back	Pungent edible bulbs	Eat at a restaurant	Ovoid foodstuff	Some small batteries (abbr)		Remains		The bones of the body	Clock face
Decay						Posed a question					
Disparage										Hits with the hand	
Cake decoration						Latin American dance; sauce					
Blackthorn fruit					Item of furniture		Loud cry				
Light brown colour				Festival							Curt
Stand up					Angers		Wizard	Make a choice			
			Fishing stick	Vast							
___ Kardashian: US celebrity		Pair of pincers		Chris ___: English singer				Official language of Pakistan	___ Hurley: English actress	___ Rida: American rapper	
Flying saucer (inits)				Envelops							
On one's ___: alone				Aseptic							
			Scarce	Metallic element	One (anag)	Roster	Cow and yak hybrid				Lazy
Female pronoun	Town ___: announcer of old						Day before Tuesday (abbr)		___ Fighters: US rock band	Bristle-like appendage	
Small restaurant or cafe								Craze			
Mary-Kate and Ashley ___: actresses	Quickly							Nocturnal bird of prey			
					A person in general						

No. 66

Immobilise	___ Maria: liqueur	Taciturn		Heavy iron blocks	Trailer	Playing card		Insect stage		Life force	Children's game (4-3-4)
				Old Testament priest		Settee					
Opposite								21st Greek letter			
						Patron saint of sailors	Stated				
Easily done	Voiles (anag)							Shrill sound	Gun	Discern; perceive	
Text message (inits)				Sort; kind				North American nation (abbr)			
Surplus	Narrow road		Explosive substance	___ Koussi: mountain in Chad				School of Mahayana Buddhism			
				Anxious							
___ Arbor: city in Michigan				Damp	___ de Ré: French island	Beginner or novice		Comment on a silly action	Gone by (of time)	Girl group who sang Waterfalls	
Foolish person							Go out with				
			City on the River Ouse				Look at amorously				
Ant and ___: TV presenters	Tremor following an earthquake										
Horse restraint	Uncooked (of meat)		Indian dish with lentils	___' Kim: US rapper	Tree of the genus Ulmus		Norwegian band (1-2)	Dialect of Chinese	___ Geller: illusionist	Amartya ___: Indian economist	Unit of energy
						Entertain					
Use to one's advantage						Employer					
Having good intentions (4-7)											

No. 67

Lhasa ___: dog breed
Corridor
Make a search
Position or point
Extent
Data transfer measure (inits)
Milky coffees
Wetland
Enjoyable

Having inherent ability
Repetition of a process
Song by two people

Escorted

Former French coin
Summer time setting (inits)
19th Greek letter

Japanese dish
Sheet (anag)

At a distance
Golf peg
Long deep track

Large vessel
Plant with fronds
Roman poet
Increase the running speed of an engine
___ Pei: breed of dog
Bases for statues

Exertion
Walk
Touch gently

Type of craftsman
The mood of a place

Reached a destination
Not new

Port in Scotland
Draw or bring out
Recede
Born

___ Rand: author
Computer core (inits)
Hind part
Paradise garden
Silly person
Layer of the eye

Call out
Turn upside down
Type of knotted pile rug
Stomach

Agitate
Egg cells

Very cold
Christmas

___ Lipa: English singer
Revoke
Rapper from New York

No. 68

Wild dog of Australia		Haughty person		Puzzle composed of many pieces		___ Campbell: Canadian actress		Sound of a hard blow	Homes		Olive ___: Popeye character
Not excusable		Fierce pal (anag)		Relax and do little		Online auction site					Gives off
Taunts						Style of rock music				Artist	
			___ Mendes: film director				Pitiless	Printer resolution (inits)			
And not	Swedish pop group		Affectedly dainty					Consume food			
Character in The Simpsons				Speaks	Country bordered by Libya and Sudan		Egyptian goddess				
Type of sandwich (inits)				Copies into an email (abbr)				Analyse	Things that may happen		Partially conceal
Wooden item used in cricket				Smack				BBC rival (inits)			
				CPU part (inits)				Sum charged			
Stride; single step	Wore away gradually							___ Lanka: island country			
Tree that bears acorns		Church service		Male swans	___ Barrett: Pink Floyd member				Clock faces	Extent of a surface	
			Capital of the Ukraine		Large salt water body		Untruth		They often have photos (abbr) (1,2)		Not wet
Grain storage chambers						Landowner					
			Perplex								
___ up: consume fully	Document allowing entry to a country					Try					

No. 69

Passage between rows of seats
Balearic party island
A knight
___ Angeles: city in California
Damp
Secretly email (inits)
Recurrent topics
Dinner jacket
Religious table
Bovine animals
Pertaining to life
Small shelter
Short note
US tax agency (inits)
Give a nickname to
Patron saint of Norway
Hard shell of a crustacean
School test
Deliberate
Threshold
One of the Seven Dwarfs
Lake or pond
Capital of Vietnam
Mother
Japanese noodle
Interdict
London district
Deities
Facsimile (abbr)
Part of a bird
Fearless and brave
Chewy substance
Excavate
Provide a substitute for
Signal for action
Primary colour
___ Camp: Barcelona's football stadium
Vehicle
Tennis score
___ Burton: US film director
Relieve or free from
Hero
Rapidity of movement
___ Sampras: tennis great
Fish
___ bread: French toast
Animal lair
Most hotel milk is this (inits)
Expression of surprise (informal)
Chris ___: British cyclist
Corrupt
Breed of dog
Picking
Argument against something
Hear a court case anew
24-hour period

No. 70

Eg male and female	Taught	Person of wealth (informal)	Fiasco		Angel of the highest order		Residue from a fire	Benicio del ___: actor		Primary time standard (inits)	Menacing
							Muslim festival	Opposite of in			
Performer of an action					Floor of a fireplace						
					Chop or cut	Anger		Text scanning process (inits)			
___ Watson: US golfer		Plant pest						Big bash	___ MacGraw: US actress	Monetary unit of Albania	
PC key		US pop star					Female sibling (informal)				
				___ Anderson: film director				Allow			
Economic stat. for a country (inits)		The first people to do something		Tolkien tree creatures	Request to turn the page (inits)	Apparition		___ Turner: US musician			
			Omar ___: US actor					Desert in central China	Diffusion of molecules through a membrane	Insect which collects pollen	
In the past	Indian state		To the ___ degree: to the utmost				Pair of actors				
			Tailless amphibian					Amartya ___: Indian economist			
Noes (anag)					Spice						
			Greek goddess of the dawn	Global commerce group (inits)				Stomach muscles (informal)		___ Bo: body fitness system	Craft orbiting the Earth (inits)
___ West: US actress	Expression of alarm				Type of carp		Italian wine region				
Lionel ___: Argentine soccer star	Tree anchors						Lack of impartiality				
					Church services						

No. 71

Aqualung		Protrudes out		Soothed		___ Del Rey: singer		Computer graphics (inits)	Continent		Garment with straps
Knowing more than one language		Flatfish of the plaice family (5,4)		US state bordered by six others		Genus of trees					Raises up
Broom made of twigs						Mixture of gases we breathe				Strangely	
			Marry				Brought to a destination	Not on			
River in eastern England	Lhasa ___: dog breed		Port city in Yemen					Place			
Small social insect				Inside information (3-3)	Japanese sport		Optical device				
23rd Greek letter				In such a manner; thus				Section of a long poem	Light boat adapted for rowing		Money given to the poor
Wet thoroughly				Rays that can damage skin (abbr)				___ Scala: actress and model			
				Adult males				Unwell			
Game played on horseback	Exertion							Athletic facility			
Legal rule		Young child		Area of a church	Long period of time				Bird homes	Ivy League university	
			Shed tears		Drunkard		Battery size		Drink a little		Longing
Alpha followers						Test or examine					
			Easily evaporated (of a substance)								
Colourant	___ Mondrian: Dutch painter					Trembling poplar					

No. 72

Tropical American tree	Excuse or pretext	Argument against something	Seabird		___ Bon Jovi: US singer		Regret with sadness	Possibility	Taxed		A poison
					Free of an obstruction						
Lie in a relaxed way							Magic spell				Hold as an opinion
Fountain pen contents				Triangular sail	Effigy	Drug that treats a disease	Eager; keen				
Insecurity		Frustrated and annoyed (3,2)	___ Henson: US puppeteer				One less than ten				
										Clay brick	
To a small extent	Sailed through		Person (informal)				Dutch cheese				
			Light toboggan	Cheek (slang)				Highly amusing thing (informal)	Absolute		Tasteless items (informal)
___-de-sac: dead end				Seed bid (anag)	Limb used for walking		Vehicle				
								Business degree (abbr)			
Type of state		___ Davis: US actress						Domestic animal			
Karaoke need (informal)	Egyptian goddess of fertility	Lawn tool						Thin fog		Drive away	Lots and lots
			Scoundrel; rogue		Eg pecan	Canine warning sound	Utter				
Money in the bank								___ Oyu: mountain			
			Length of time something lasts								
Child		Hear a court case anew						Lean-___: simple shelters			

No. 73

- Hard green gem
- _/__ carte: menu type (1,2)
- Discernible
- Pertaining to the mind
- Type of computer
- Gave a meal to
- Russian sovereign
- One (Spanish)
- Contriving to bring about
- Dry (of wine)
- Follow on from
- ___ oil: product of the flax plant
- ___ Arbor: city in Michigan
- Edward ___: English poet
- Tailless amphibian
- Squanders
- Equipment for fishing
- ___ John: English singer
- Letters at the end of page one (inits)
- Most hotel milk is this (inits)
- Lubricate
- ___ Aviv: city in Israel
- Joke
- Capita of Latvia
- Paul ___: former England footballer
- South African political party (inits)
- Widely cultivated cereal grass
- Definite article
- Market a product
- Religious sister
- Port in Scotland
- ___ es Salaam: city in Tanzania
- Among
- Beam of light
- Muhammad ___: boxing great
- Male person
- Large insect
- ___ Malek: US actor
- Tropical starchy tuber
- ___ Rickman: English actor
- Opposite of no
- Appalling
- Discussion
- Organ of hearing
- High mountain
- Rocky peak
- Female sheep
- Direction opposite NNW
- Criticise strongly
- Not in
- Silvery fish of the carp family
- Protective cover
- Ruin
- Permit
- ___ Arabia: country
- Stood for

No. 74

Part of a coat		Involving space and time (4-11)	Evergreen coniferous tree		Sandy ___: Scottish golfer		Treat indulgently	Summer time setting (inits)	Pain in a person's belly (7,4)	Blade for rowing a boat	Eg Oxfam (inits)
Doubtful					More likely than not (4-2)						
							Adult male deer				
Marred	Midge ___: Ultravox musician				Sheet of floating ice		Benicio del ___: actor				
Tacks on	Haul		Engage in argument	___ Rida: American rapper				Pained cry		Hawaiian dish made from taro root	Financiers
				Monetary unit of Romania				Software program (abbr)			
Tear				___ and Zag: puppet duo		Chocolate powder					
Confound						___ Pound: US poet		Smack			
One of the Spice Girls					Towards a ship's stern		Animal enclosure	Twisted to one side		Female pronoun	
Des ___: desirable house (informal)	Get away from		Cold Spanish tomato soup								
			Gastropod	Spruce up							
Female sibling (informal)				Large ships							
Arguments against					Texter's digression (inits)	Chris ___: English singer	Slip up		Climbing vine	The Matrix role	___ up on: find out about
___ Ivanovic: tennis star				Making beer							
Artist								Shape formed by flying geese			
Measure of length				State of armed conflict				Over there (literary)			

No. 75

Now and then		Becomes less severe	East	Eminem song featuring Dido	Swedish airline	Having a liking for		Paces		Forceful blow	___ Friel: English actress
Annoyed						City in Japan					
An assured fact										Quartzlike gems	
Assumed name						Evil spirit					
Observed					Pours freely (of water)		Father				
Pub			US state								Transmits
Bus driver in The Simpsons					Dreadful		Opening for air; outlet	Ernie ___: South African golfer			
			Increase the running speed of an engine	Varied							
Outs opposite		Gave way to pressure		Frozen water				Far from difficult	Global commerce group (inits)	Slippery fish	
Strong alkaline solution				Revitalised							
___ Tyler: actress				Large areas of land							
			Currency of Spain and Holland	Great tennis serves	Pouch; enclosed space	___ James: US singer	Basic monetary unit of Peru				Fibber
Affirmative vote	Let						Psychic ability (inits)		Beer	Large extinct flightless bird	
Teach								Friend (French)			
Renown	Constructs a building							Mauna ___: Hawaiian volcano			
					Seem						

No. 76

Upward slopes

Cave dweller's time (5,3)

Harsh cry of a crow

Graceful in form

Free of an obstruction

Id ___: that is to say

Skilfully; adeptly

___ Koussi: mountain in Chad

Perilously

Animal fodder

River bottom

Mineral powder

___ Barlow: English actress

Of a dull brownish colour

Zodiac sign

Opposite of yang

Speech sound

Devout

Method; fashion

Rotten (of food)

Pair of performers

Central

Fever

Large beer cask

Word expressing negation

Soft animal hair

Cry of a cat

Grew frail

Gull-like bird

Nip (anag)

Gives life to

___ Fighters: US rock band

Total spread of a bridge

Nocturnal birds of prey

If

Back muscle (informal)

___ Stubbs: English actress

Signal assent with the head

One's family

Very small child

An individual thing

___ David: US lyricist

Green vegetable

Small portion or share

___ de Ré: French island

Inform upon

Gene material

Monstrous humanoid creature

Great sorrow

Lyric poem

Nothing (informal)

Greek letters

Sailing vessel

Walks through water

Select class

Roman emperor

Rare

No. 77

Burkina ___: African country	Capable of being done	Noise		Shaped up	Drinking tube	Era (anag)	Shipyard worker		In such a manner; thus		Causing difficulties
				Indian garment					Riches		Ridge of rock
Snake											
Gradation of colour				___ Varney: English actor				Herb; regret			
Country in southern Asia						Church farmland					
			___ Egan: Westlife singer	River in Wales				___ Ramsey: football manager			
Marry		What you walk on		___ Blyton: writer	Untruth	Deceptive manoeuvre					Helper
Far away from home							Small hollows in a surface	North American nation (abbr)			
Men's tight fitting hat							___ and cons: pluses and minuses				
Not strict								River in Germany			
			Nine plus one		Surprise result		City on the River Ouse	Type of baleen whale			
Animal doctor	Large tuna	Baby beds		Employs					Courts	Repeat	
Excellent serve				Slip up		Golf peg		Damp			
Veracity								Plant related to wood sorrel			
			Enclosure for sheep (in Scotland)				Fourth Gospel				
Blue ___: bird	Arranged by type							Drunkard			

No. 78

Use inefficiently	Arcade game pioneer	Replace	American girl group		___ Nishikori: Japanese tennis star		Opposite of downs	Avoids	Large insect		Push back
					Portions						
Spring flowers							One given red-carpet treatment (inits)				Long grass
As easy as ___: simple				Toothed wheel	Roman poet	Ursine	Genus of trees				
Found		Flower part; pales (anag)	Hazelnut				___ Steyn: South African bowler				
										Pried	
Plant liquid	Small pointed tools		___ Scala: actress and model				Beach constituent				
			Repeated jazz phrase	___ Hill: US R&B group				Silence	Opened a wine bottle		Opposite of cold
State of armed conflict				Slow mover	Musical instrument (informal)		___ Barrett: Pink Floyd member				
								The Matrix role			
Dots indicating an omission		Unreliable						Chicago's summer time zone (inits)			
Extra postscript (inits)	Mountain top	Deceived						Imaginary monsters		Italian greeting	Snag (anag)
			Speak; state		Cause friction	___ Geller: illusionist	Annual car test (inits)				
Tympanic membrane								South Korean car maker			
			Eg from Italy or Spain								
Put down		Circle a planet						Man's best friend			

No. 79

Tracey ___: English artist

Charter signed by King John (5,5)

Creative thoughts

Speed in nautical miles per hour

Kingdom

Web access company (inits)

Television surface

___-haw: donkey sound

Car pedal

Stand up

Failing to give proper care

Seek (anag)

Youth

Acquire; obtain

Fourth month (abbr)

Expression of alarm

Of the nose

Large bird of prey

Document allowing entry to a country

One of the Three Stooges

___ Dennis: TV presenter

Used to be

Pavement edge

Intellectual faculty

Science subject degree (abbr) (1,2)

Film ___: gritty film genre

Maze

With hands on the hips

Opposite one of two

___ Gadot: Israeli actress

Oppose

Second Greek letter

Share; portion

Person of wealth (informal)

Gave a meal to

Customary

Become firm

Attempt to do

Taxi

Possible URL ending

Cow meat

___ Major: the Great Bear

Current units, briefly

Ark builder

'Officer' order of chivalry (inits)

Sphere or globe

Farewell remark

___ DiFranco: US singer

Enclosed fortification

Day before Tuesday (abbr)

Beam of light

Petty quarrel

Epoch

Legendary; mythical

'Be quiet!'

No. 80

Open up

Art ___: design style

Spanish rice dish

___ Duncan Smith: politician

Summer time setting (inits)

Morals

Camera type (inits)

Science of biological processes

Well timed

Type of earring

A son of Adam and Eve

Bonds of union

Reel for winding yarn

To the ___ degree: to the utmost

European deer

Blind salamander

Spiced mixture of fruits

Annoy

Ninth month (abbr)

Queen of Carthage in Virgil's Aeneid

Unpleasant sensation

Seb ___: British former athlete

Dr ___: US rapper and record producer

Calls to mind

Spiced tea

Exploits

BBC rival (inits)

Copies into an email (abbr)

Growl with bare teeth

Me (humorous)

Wets (anag)

Pair of performers

Female chicken

Greek letter 'M's

Shola ___: singer

Tenth month (abbr)

Cry of a goose

Creepier

___ Turner: US musician

Clumsy person

Strongbox

Send down a ball in cricket

CPU part (inits)

Join together

Give up one's rights

Strong criticism

___ & Stimpy: US animated sitcom

___ Ramsey: football manager

___ Jones: US stock index

Large black dung beetle

Surface upon which one walks

Assisted

Moderately rich (4-2-2)

___ culpa

Oven or furnace

Less

No. 81

Made in bulk (4-8)		Highest singing voice	Spoof	Apple tablet	Bed for a baby	Individual article or unit		Stand up		Line joining corners of a square	Takes an exam
Savoury jelly						Follows closely					
Ongoing television serial (4,5)										Hoarse	
Small marine fish						Strength					
Push; poke					Journeys by sea		___-chef: kitchen's number two				
Physics unit				Multiples of twelve							___ Agassi: former tennis star
Variety of agate					Long flowing hair		Argues	Alias initials			
			___ Hart: English goalkeeper	___ Monroe: famous actress							
Wedding words (1,2)		Cause to absorb water		Before the present				Legendary creature	Brian ___: Roxy Music musician	High value playing card	
___ Oyu: mountain				This starts on 1st January (3,4)							
Organ of sight				Vital content							
			Spoken test	Broadcasts	Toothed wheel	Shades; tones	Foot extremity				Sailors
Eccentric; strange	Fish of the carp family						Home for a pig		Sooty's girlfriend	Dessert (informal)	
More than one								Health resort			
Head over ___: totally (in love)	Victim							Belonging to us			
					Church councils						

No. 82

Acer tree

Pertaining to bees

___ Pot: Khmer Rouge leader

Monetary unit of Albania

Wager

Ethereal

African antelope

Collect or store

Scope or extent

Complex problem

Metrical writing

Queen ___: fairy in Romeo and Juliet

Intellectual faculty

Sort; kind

Implore

Line Earth rotates around

Confused mixture

Proper

Rigid

Ultimate

Sound of a hard blow

Not in favour

Snow home

Longing

Seal of the Archbishop of York

Loose white judo jackets

Parched

Eg Andrew Motion

'Be quiet!'

Tranquil

Appetising drink

Dialect of Chinese

Bread roll

Tough animal tissue

Piece of cloth

Came across

Hawaiian dish made from taro root

Flat image that looks 3D

Wipe

Long period of time

Seventh month (abbr)

Not new

Taut

Lean

Vein of metal ore

Affectedly dainty

Auction item

Consume food

Snow runner

___ Danson: US actor

Least hard

Haul

Elks idea (anag)

By now

Stinky

Sum charged

No. 83

Herb	Purple quartz	Tear	Ice statues with coal for eyes		Happy; carefree		___ Rand: author	Brass musical instrument		Wet soil	Affiliation
							US tax agency (inits)	___ Thurman: actress			
Short skirt					Type of rain cloud						
					Pub	Breed of dog		Eg website banners (informal)			
Storage place		Hits with a lash						Circular storage medium	Unwell	Way to up website views (inits)	
Computer memory unit		List of food options					Widely cultivated cereal grass				
				Eg Oxfam (inits)				Garland of flowers			
Pickup vehicle in Australia		Fortify against attack		Manure	Type of savings account (abbr)	Relating to time		Mauna ___: Hawaiian volcano			
			___ Romney: US politician					Round before the final (abbr)	Endless	Sound of a cow	
Woman's first public appearance (informal)	Ate (anag)		Exploit unfairly				Type of statistical chart				
			Temporary living quarters					Also			
Mission					Clay ___: shooting target						
			CPU part (inits)	Female deer				Fully		Half of four	Psychic ability (inits)
Vessel	___ Dalyell: former politician				___ West: US actress		Poker stake				
Wait in line	Camel-like animal						Rules of a country				
					Move with a bounding motion						

No. 84

Rope with a running noose	Heavy iron tool	Perceive	One more than five		Record		Two (Spanish)	Long essay	Princely		Asian pepper plant
					Stableman						
Equine sounds							Head covering				Plant stalk
Annoy				Cook in hot oil	Dutch cheese	Opposite of a promotion	Days before major events				
Heraldic lily (5-2-3)		Loosened	Gave a meal to				River sediment				
										Simple aquatic plants	
Possesses	Among		Sweet potato				Fraud				
			Puts down; produces eggs	Gang				Type of starch	Church of England member		Choose
___ Gibson: US actor				Prisoner	Definite article		Bed for a baby				
								Short sleep			
Intended to teach		Loutish person						Acquire; obtain			
Collection of paper	Basic unit of matter	Used up						Team		Facts and statistics collectively	Garden of ___: biblical place
			Small crow		Lipid	Influenza	Drink a little				
Duties or taxes								Scoundrel			
			Confirm								
In what way		Scheme intended to deceive (3-2)						Type of leavened bread			

No. 85

Type of hairstyle	Stair pulls (anag)	Plummeted		Absolute	Bungle	__/_ whole: in general (2,1)	Jumped up		Not inspiring; apathetic (informal)		Stretch out completely
				Support or foundation					Having luxurious tastes		Compass point
Outer part of the earth											
Rays that can damage skin (abbr)				Bitumen				Small green vegetable			
Ancient object						Operatic songs					
			Thomas ___: German author	Female chicken				Chicago's summer time zone (inits)			
Father		Type of wood		Norse god	___ Gershwin: lyricist	Adhesive					Fruiting body of a fungus
Sloping (of a typeface)							Freight	Inform upon			
Spanish title for a married woman							Toy block brand				
Drinking vessel								_/__ carte: menu type (1,2)			
			Flat-topped conical hat		Contented cat sounds		Greek letter 'M's	___ Beatty: US actor			
Put a question to	Be in debt	Sever with the teeth		Splendid display					Mark or blemish	Sea eagle	
'Officer' order of chivalry (inits)				___ Titmuss: TV personality		Comment on a silly action		Become firm			
Magicians								In favour of			
			Male sibling (informal)				Lead singer of U2				
Animal doctor	___ Cuthbert: Kim Bauer in 24							___ Aviv: city in Israel			

No. 86

Morally wicked	Compete for	Failure to understand		Opposite of an acid	Pertaining to the liver	Be unwell		Radio code word for 'P'		Small batteries (abbr)	Stealthy
				Very powerful arms (inits)		___ Newton: scientist					
Writing fluid holder								Friend			
						Female child	US space agency				
Depart suddenly	Late time of life (3,3)							Gets less difficult	French friend	One of the Seven Dwarfs	
Obesity scale (inits)				___ Maria: liqueur				Increase in amount			
Thread	Performs in a play		And not	US tax agency (inits)				Bartender in The Simpsons			
				Clergymen							
Business leader (inits)				Deciduous tree	Muslim festival	Cook slowly in liquid		Every	Former French coin	___ Dalyell: former politician	
Trios							Italian wine region				
			Ignited				Give temporarily				
Exploit unfairly	Pen name (3,2,5)										
Emergency priority system	Type of knotted pile rug		Ruction	___ up on: find out about	City on the River Ouse		To and ___: from place to place	Monetary unit of Romania	Stomach muscles (informal)	Hair product	Wily
						Grows weary					
Ye old (anag)						Insurgent					
Without giving a name											

No. 87

Man (informal)		Pulled apart		East ___: where one finds Norfolk		Halt		Regret with sadness	Cowers (anag)		French for 'salt'
Bravely		Reluctant		European mountain range		Woody plant					Shows tiredness
Ring						Chest muscle (informal)				Absolutely incredible	
			___ chart: type of graph				Pleasure	Uncooked (of meat)			
Not many	Hairstyle of tight curls		Gus Van ___: film director					Possess			
Key next to the space bar				Pressing keys	Tie		Is indebted to pay				
Small winged insect				Large black dung beetle				Fully prepared	Person (informal)		Grows older
Tear				Cereal grass				Tropical constrictor			
				Shola ___: singer				'Goodness me!' online (inits)			
___ Morrison: US novelist	Chewed like a rodent							River in Scotland			
Apple computer		Taxis		Where darts players throw from	Greek goddess of the night				Vascular tissue in plants	Stringed instrument	
			Applaud		Australian singer and songwriter		___ Guevara: guerrilla leader		Sphere or globe		Rocky peak
Voting groups						Hit hard					
			Until now								
Type of savings account (abbr)	Earnest appeal					Remnant of a dying fire					

No. 88

Third Greek letter	Mingle with something else	Large extinct flightless bird	Blend together		Disallow		Form of public transport	Surprise results	Examine again		More recent
					Loan shark						
Activities							Long bench				Noble gas
Mad ___: Mel Gibson film				Relax; do nothing (informal)	Flag lily	Complete	Reindeer in Frozen				
Aggravate; make worse		Debate in a heated manner	By way of				Gaelic name for Ireland				
										Stadium	
Implore	Light fawn colour		Loose white judo jackets				White aquatic bird				
			Male sheep (pl)	Weep				Lyric poems	Certificates of education		Hit high into the air
Aggressive dog				Use up; exhaust	Not near		Strong alkaline solution				
								Fountain pen contents			
Terrible		Fleshy						Make good on a debt			
Owns	Highly excited	Shopping binge						US state bordered by six others		Desire; hope for	Tray (anag)
			Bulge downwards under pressure		River in Wales	Software program (abbr)	Opposite of no				
Entrance								Russian space station			
			Always in a similar role (of an actor)								
Pig		Looks furtively						Timid			

No. 89

Deciduous coniferous tree | Link a town with another | Shooting star | True information | Legal rule | Woman's garment | ___ David: US lyricist

In a creative manner | Insipid and bland | Not hard | Jessica ___: actress | Loutish person

Small boat | One more than one | Movement conveying an expression

Pro | Readily recovering from shock | Word used to express disgust

Videotape letters (inits) | Slender freshwater fish | Arduous journey | Way to up website views (inits)

___ Lynam: TV presenter | Having pimples | Large bag | Pose (anag)

High mountain | In such a manner; thus | Conflict | Sewn edge | Chickens lay these

Business leader (inits) | Entirely | Gradation of colour

US spy agency (inits) | Unit of energy

Greatest | Posts driven into the ground | ___ Ryan: US actress

Tropical starchy tuber | Large South American rodent | Metric unit of mass | Healthcare provider (inits) | Took illegally | Costa ___: Central American country

Pulp | Pub | ___ Danson: US actor | Pen point | Road vehicle

Island in the Bay of Naples | Medicine

Aromatic plant used in cooking

Step in dancing | Church song | Suspend; prevent

No. 90

Gradual reduction in value
Direct or control
Purify
Proper
___ up: agitated
Go out with
Extent or limit
Languid
Island of the Inner Hebrides
Transform bit by bit
Zodiac sign
Gilbert and Sullivan works
Send payment
Renovate; refurbish
Way in
Slender
Assign
Merriment
___ McKellen: English actor
Respect and admire
Slight hollows in a surface
Let it stand
Jelly or culture medium
Small mountain lake
___ Vicious: Sex Pistols member
The opposite of downs
A dancer or singer
Abu Dhabi's location (inits)
Small spot
___ Scala: actress and model
Volcano in Sicily
Battery size
Wily
Web access company (inits)
Alongside each other
Wife of Saturn
Antlers (anag)
Narrow inlets
Corner
Much ___ About Nothing: play
Sound a cat makes
Negative vote
Saw; observed
Single in number
Dairy product
Gene material
Wager
Guitar with four strings (abbr)
Lost grip
Purchase
Large waterbirds
Isolated inlet of the sea
___ out: be frugal with
Remained expectantly

No. 91

Partly open	Activity of writing articles	Plant pest		Crown documents	Top degree mark	___ Reed: US musician	Historical records		Seventh Greek letter		Makes better
				Apartment					Lateness		___ Winton: TV presenter
Dogmatic											
Most hotel milk is this (inits)				Flee				_/__ carte: menu type (1,2)			
Exposes to danger						___ Lavigne: Canadian singer					
			Queen in Frozen	___ Aviv: city in Israel				Female kangaroo			
Cease		At some point in the past		Solitary	Ancient	Agitate					Stargazing instrument
Move with a bounding motion							Jewel from an oyster shell	___ King Cole: US jazz pianist			
Instep							___ Sampras: tennis great				
Thing causing outrage								French for 'salt'			
			Take to court		Stadium		Ethereal	Direction opposite NNW			
Former music magazine	And so on (abbr)	Hew		___ Romeo: car					Tells an untruth	___ Sandler: comedian	
Former term for euro				Edge of a cup		Of a low standard		Varnish resin			
Thus; as a result								Wedding words (1,2)			
			_/_ jiffy: very soon (2,1)				Pile				
Umberto ___: author	Scented ointment							Company with under 500 staff (inits)			

No. 92

Momentary oversight
Arcade game pioneer
Hawaiian dish made from taro root
Add together
Domestic animal
Soil; dirt
Pressed clothes
Parody
Start
Suitable for all
Solicited business
Piece of cloth
Badger's home
Goal
Vocation
Eager; keen
Defector
___ Redding: US singer
Person who finds something
Church council
Jolt
One less than ten
Leaf of parchment
___ Solo: Star Wars character
Genus of trees
Rubbish container
Neatly skilful; agile
Video game company
Kapil ___: Indian cricketer
Chat
Distresses
Soviet security police (inits)
Variety of lettuce
Japanese dish of raw fish
Ram
___ Harding: Welsh actor
Soft fruit with seeds
Base of a statue
Overly showy
Chain attached to a watch
Sharp blow
Small berrylike fruit
Trembling poplar
___ Hadid: US fashion model
Greek goddess of the Earth
Paul ___: former England footballer
Flexible container
Unit of weight
Along with; also
Put down
Wealth
Is able to
Main cost (anag)
Witch
Breezy
Stamped letter enclosure (inits)

No. 93

Greet	Infinite time	Scientific workplace (abbr)	Military expedition		Ten raised to the power 100		___ Lynam: TV presenter	Alan ___: US actor		Heavy stove	Depletion of bodily fluids
							___-jong: Chinese game	Boy			
Tropical Asian plant					Smear or blur						
					Word used to express disgust	___ chi		Sound of relief			
Remove errors from software		Opposite of north						Move fast in a straight line	Edible mushroom	Abu Dhabi's location (inits)	
Posterior		Simple aquatic organism					Ernie ___: golfer				
				Go quickly (archaic)				Organ of hearing			
Port in Scotland		Withdraws		Heroic poem	Physics unit	Frozen dessert (3,5)		Legume			
			Dwarf planet					Indian garment	Canvas shelters	Friend of Tigger	
Key next to the space bar	Garland of flowers		___-Man: classic arcade game				Small batteries (abbr)				
			Thought or suggestion					Court			
___ Clapton: English guitarist					Large artillery gun						
			Large tuna	Title of a married woman				Greek goddess of the dawn		___ Gershwin: lyricist	___ Amitri: Scottish band
By way of	Low bank of coral				By now		___ Blyton: writer				
Suggest	Eighth Greek letter						Mythical giant				
					Prayer book						

No. 94

Induce fear

Breed of dog

Residue; type of tree

___ Ferdinand: footballer

Sum charged

They prove who you are (abbr) (1,2)

Slice of bacon

Swimming costume

Lowest point

Seaport in South Africa

Willow twigs

Assist

Emperor of Rome 54-68

17th Greek letter

Wager

Country whose capital is Vientiane

Trying to heal

This covers your body

Dispirit

Small seat

Type of sandwich (inits)

Rent

Christmas song

The sound of a dove

Nocturnal birds of prey

Foot extremity

Puerto ___: Caribbean island

Bites at

___ Paulo: city in Brazil

Edible fat

Appetising drink

___ Leppard: rock band

Came first in a race

Pledge

Droop

Hit high into the air

Edgar Allan ___: US writer

Dots indicating an omission

Silly trick

Small sprite

___ Mahal: mausoleum at Agra

From a distance

Dank

Japanese food paste

Settee

Large antelope

Pitcher

Lubricate

___ Thurman: Kill Bill actress

Secret agent

Livid

Hill

Make less complex

Periodic publication (abbr)

Interruption

Facsimile (abbr)

No. 95

Small place of refuge
Wealth
Greek letters
Leader of a community
Part of the eye
Stream of liquid
Joan ___: Spanish artist
___ Brown: US author
Act of freeing from blame
Friendly greeting
Silvery fish of the carp family
Platform leading out to sea
Chest
Cause friction
Ballpoint pen brand
Yoko ___: Japanese artist
___ Sarandon: US actress
Local sporting match
Donated
Increase in amount
Small truck
___ Taylor-Joy: actress
Hawaiian island
Mountain pass
Secretly email (inits)
___ es Salaam: city in Tanzania
Evergreen coniferous tree
Breadth
A man
Pull at
Grandiosity of language
Genetic make-up (inits)
PC key
Country where one finds Bamako
Person devoted to love
Opposite of high
Roll of bank notes
Consumed food
What did you say?
Female pronoun
Matures
Sound of a cow
Interim office worker
Unseated by a horse
___ Luhrmann: film director
___ Hart: English goalkeeper
Cooking utensil
Fully
Enemy
___ Goodman: dance judge
Recede
However
Edith ___: French singer
Franz ___: Hungarian composer
___ Arabia: country
Capital of Norway
Bovine animals

No. 96

- Draw or bring out
- Method of learning by repetition
- Wrist bone
- Rolled up tortilla sandwich
- Mauna ___: Hawaiian volcano
- Caress
- Huge mythical bird
- Type of sweet
- Actors
- Auditory receptors
- Too
- Lyres
- Not expensive
- Blade for rowing a boat
- Bodies of writing
- UK air force (abbr)
- Prescient
- Text scanning process (inits)
- Insect
- Eg bullets (abbr)
- Smack with the hand
- Area of seating at Liverpool FC
- Suitable
- Island of the South Pacific
- ___ mater: your old school
- Belonging to a woman
- ___ Farrow: US actress
- Donkey
- Fight (3-2)
- Give a nickname to
- Female chickens
- ___-jong: Chinese game
- Sheltered side
- Comment on a silly action
- Came across
- Midge ___: Ultravox musician
- ___ Morrison: US novelist
- Narrow passage of water
- Disallow
- Variety of lettuce
- Neither good nor bad (2-2)
- Rain (anag)
- Eleventh month (abbr)
- Battery units
- Assistant
- Short tail
- Small winged insect
- US spy agency (inits)
- Diving bird
- Cry of a cat or gull
- Neck warmer
- Assertion
- Height
- ___ Reed: US musician
- Very small
- Awry; lopsided

No. 97

Gull-like bird	Olive-green mountain parrot	Taciturn		Al ___: US actor	Royal houses	Young newt		Small body of water		Herb	Group of islands
				Third eyelid in some mammals		Plants of a region					
Bewitch								Belonging to us			
						Actor's part in a film	___ Stewart: ex-England cricketer				
Cosmetic treatment	Ahead							Triangular river mouth	Spoil	Large primate	
Style of rock music				Seb ___: British former athlete				___ tai: cocktail			
Liquid food	Use these to row a boat		Adobe file format	Measure of length				Software program (abbr)			
				Release from captivity (3,4)							
Along with; also				US crime fighters (inits)	Varnish resin	Modify		Possess	South Korean car maker	Relieve or free from	
Shuffle playing cards							Green vegetable				
			Of a low standard				Kristen ___: US actress				
Computer key	Expert on a subject										
Airships	Was in first place		Not inspiring; apathetic (informal)	Be nosy	___ Barrett: Pink Floyd member		Heavy stove	Allow	___ DiFranco: US singer	___ Ferdinand: footballer	Adult males
						Warning sound					
All						Spirit in a bottle					
Hinder today (anag)											

No. 98

Tibetan Buddhist monk
Lingering visual impression
Lament
In a slow tempo (of music)
Survived
Rays that can damage skin (abbr)
Alcove
Female chicken
Agent who supplies goods to stores
Entice
Placed in the care of
Fraud
Absolution
Pull at
Hoover (abbr)
To the ___ degree: to the utmost
Decay
Additional; excess
Puerto ___: Caribbean island
___ Kapital: Karl Marx work
Edge of a cup
Type of vase
Spots
Quantity of medication
Id ___: that is to say
Rebuff
Thing with no special qualities
Unmarried young woman
Makhaya ___: South African cricketer
What our planet orbits
Address a person boldly
Bus driver in The Simpsons
Costing (anag)
Very long time
Many times (literary)
Flatten on impact
___ favor: please (Spanish)
Dr ___: US record producer
Sum charged
Monstrous humanoid creature
Abstain from food
Drinks a little
Plant with an edible root
Bone of the forearm
Not on
Explosive substance
Inflated feeling of pride
However
Type of snake (informal)
Old Testament priest
Annoy constantly
US monetary unit
Copies into an email (abbr)
Stain skin with indelible colour
Scotland's longest river

No. 99

Compete for		Discernible	Before (literary)		Become dim		Relays (anag)	Sprite	Process of clotting; curdling	Charged particle	Small social insect
Thought or suggestion					___ Keys: US singer						
							Earth's satellite				
Strangely	Perceive with the eyes				A lyric poet		Breathe hard				
Frozen rain	Matured		Carries with effort	Garment with straps				One of the continents		Ninth month (abbr)	Ingenuous
				Donkey				North American nation (abbr)			
Large dark antelope				And so on (abbr)		Lazy person; layabout					
___ on: urged to do						TV award		Suitable			
Fine powder					Final line on an agenda (inits)		Hog	___ Dogg: US rapper		Day after Mon. (abbr)	
Title of a married woman	Stole from		Where tents are pitched								
			Bird of the parrot family	Foreboding							
Unit of resistance				Past events							
Sheep sounds					Pickup vehicle in Australia	Chemical element	Plant related to wood sorrel		___ de Ré: French island	Trouble in mind or body	Greek letter 'N's
Airer of Doctor Who (inits)				Idealistic							
Flexible								Lucy ___: US actress			
Water droplets formed at night				Aunt ___: Bambi character				Ernie ___: South African golfer			

No. 100

Move fast in a straight line	Young bear	Basic		Farewells	Vent for molten lava	Cash dispenser (inits)		Chopped; cancelled		Frozen water	Not absolute
				Fish appendage		Poisonous					
Identifying outfit								Umberto ___: author			
						At any time	Port city in Yemen				
Descend down a cliff	Snow leopards							Silk fabric	Parent / teacher group (inits)	Cut of pork	
Extra postscript (inits)				___ Gardner: US actress				21st Greek letter			
Modify	Shallow food container		Your (poetic)	Tennis court divider				Tasteless items (informal)			
				Japanese art of paper folding							
To some extent (informal)				___ Gibson: US actor	Unwell	Israeli airline (2,2)		Popular Oxford degree (inits)	Mixture of gases we breathe	Once ___/_ blue moon: rarely (2,1)	
Obstruct							Unpleasant sensation				
			Former measure of length				___ colada: cocktail				
Large tuna	Security for a loan										
Rich cake	Type of beer		___ de Cologne: perfume	Part of a curve	___ Stubbs: English actress		Garland of flowers	Ab ___: from the very beginning	___ Diesel: US actor	Greek letter	Indian lentil stew
						Cherished					
Acquire knowledge of						Andrew Lloyd Webber musical					
Serving to enlighten; instructive											

No. 1

	S			W		V					
	P	I	S	A		A	B	A	C	U	S
R	A	N	K	I	N	G		B	U	S	H
		C	A	T		U		I	S	P	Y
		O			D	E	B		T		
T	A	M	P		O	R	E		O	B	I
	A	P	U		R		L	E	M	O	N
	A	R	R	A	Y		T		B	A	T
	S	E	E	R		U			U		O
		H		C	A	N	A	D	I	A	N
O	L	E			B	I	V	A	L	V	E
	E	N	A		E	X	A	C	T	E	D
	A	S	P	S				H			
	N	I	P		U	N	E	A	R	T	H
	T	O	L	S	T	O	Y		Y	O	U
	O	N	E		E	V	E		E	G	G

No. 2

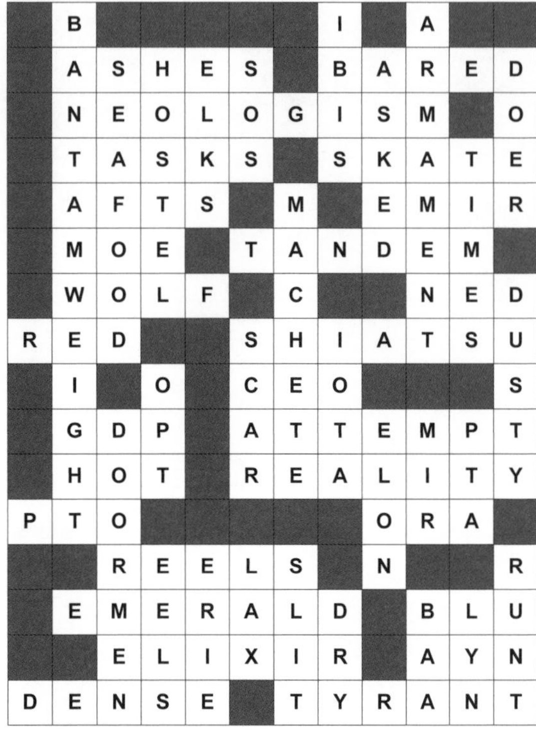

	B						I		A		
	A	S	H	E	S		B	A	R	E	D
	N	E	O	L	O	G	I	S	M		O
	T	A	S	K	S		S	K	A	T	E
	A	F	T	S		M		E	M	I	R
	M	O	E		T	A	N	D	E	M	
	W	O	L	F		C			N	E	D
R	E	D			S	H	I	A	T	S	U
	I		O		C	E	O				S
	G	D	P		A	T	T	E	M	P	T
	H	O	T		R	E	A	L	I	T	Y
P	T	O						O	R	A	
		R	E	E	L	S		N			R
	E	M	E	R	A	L	D		B	L	U
		E	L	I	X	I	R		A	Y	N
D	E	N	S	E		T	Y	R	A	N	T

No. 3

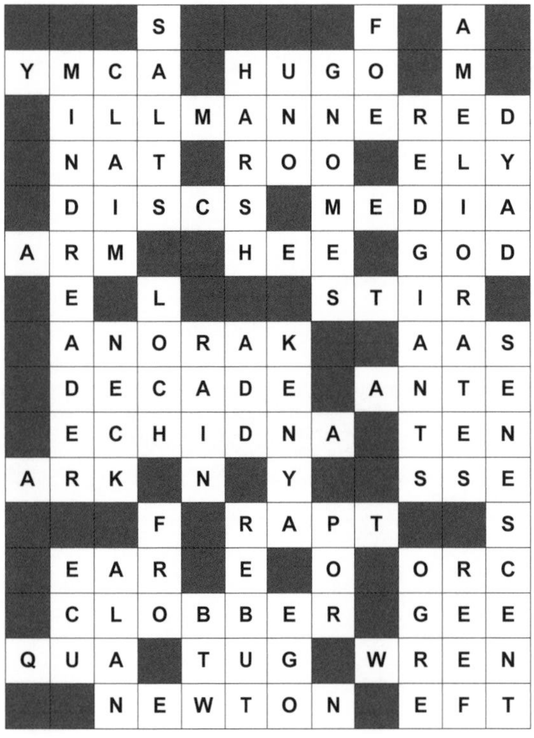

			S					F		A	
Y	M	C	A		H	U	G	O		M	
	I	L	L	M	A	N	N	E	R	E	D
	N	A	T		R	O	O		E	L	Y
	D	I	S	C	S		M	E	D	I	A
A	R	M			H	E	E		G	O	D
	E		L				S	T	I	R	
	A	N	O	R	A	K			A	A	S
	D	E	C	A	D	E		A	N	T	E
	E	C	H	I	D	N	A		T	E	N
A	R	K		N		Y			S	S	E
			F		R	A	P	T			S
	E	A	R		E		O		O	R	C
	C	L	O	B	B	E	R		G	E	E
Q	U	A		T	U	G		W	R	E	N
		N	E	W	T	O	N		E	F	T

No. 4

				T		B				B	
C	A	C	T	I		U	N	I	S	O	N
	U	R	A	N	U	S		S	I	X	
	D	U	N					S	E	E	P
	I			G	I	S		U	R	D	U
J	O	L	L	Y	R	O	G	E	R		L
		O		P	O	L		S	A	I	L
R	A	T			N	I	X			G	
	G	U	S			T		K	I	L	O
W	A	S	T	E	F	U	L		N	O	W
	R		O	X	I	D	E		T	O	N
			A	C	T	E	D		R		
G	E	M		L				M	E	T	E
	R	O	T	U	N	D	A		P	U	G
D	O	T		D	O	U	B	L	I	N	G
	S		C	E	D	E	S		D	A	S

No. 5

			S					G		D	
E	D	I	E		D	U	T	Y		E	
	E	N	L	A	R	G	E	M	E	N	T
	A	T	M		O	H	M		D	O	E
	T	R	A	I	N		P	L	U	M	E
R	H	O			E	V	E		C	I	D
	W		L				R	O	A	N	
	A	R	I	A	N	A			T	A	T
	T	O	R	P	O	R		Z	I	T	I
	C	R	A	S	H	E	S		N	O	T
T	H	Y		O		A			G	R	R
			V		E	S	P	Y			A
	B	A	A		R		P		H	E	T
	O	B	L	O	N	G	S		U	Z	I
N	A	B		R	I	P		A	F	R	O
		A	B	B	E	S	S		F	A	N

No. 6

	A						O		M		
	P	A	T	E	R		T	S	A	R	S
	P	R	O	V	I	D	I	N	G		U
	R	I	L	E	D		S	I	N	C	E
	E	D	E	N		V		P	A	R	T
	H	I	D		S	I	E	S	T	A	
	E	T	O	N		L			E	V	A
A	N	Y			A	L	I	A	S	E	S
	S		E		I	A	N				T
	I	F	S		D	I	F	F	U	S	E
	V	E	T		S	N	O	O	K	E	R
L	E	E						N	E	W	
		L	I	T	H	E		T			D
	F	I	R	E	A	R	M		W	H	O
		N	A	S	S	A	U		O	U	T
S	I	G	N	S		S	M	O	K	E	S

No. 7

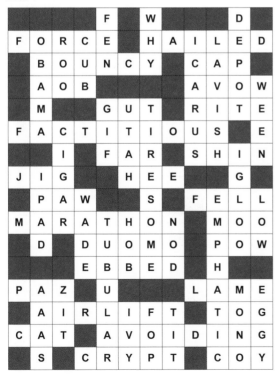

				F		W				D	
F	O	R	C	E		H	A	I	L	E	D
	B	O	U	N	C	Y		C	A	P	
	A	O	B					A	V	O	W
	M			G	U	T		R	I	T	E
F	A	C	T	I	T	I	O	U	S		E
		I		F	A	R		S	H	I	N
J	I	G			H	E	E			G	
	P	A	W			S		F	E	L	L
M	A	R	A	T	H	O	N		M	O	O
	D		D	U	O	M	O		P	O	W
			E	B	B	E	D		H		
P	A	Z		U				L	A	M	E
	A	I	R	L	I	F	T		T	O	G
C	A	T		A	V	O	I	D	I	N	G
	S		C	R	Y	P	T		C	O	Y

No. 8

	O		R		V		B			K	
	S		O		I		A	C	A	I	
E	A	U	D	E	C	O	L	O	G	N	E
	K	N	E	L	T		M	B	A		T
Z	A	C		M	I	G			S	H	H
		H		S	M	E	E		S	O	O
	W	A	S			N		O	I	L	S
	I	R	K		T	E	A			D	
	P	T	A		A	R	C		C	A	N
M	E	E	T		P	A	T		O	L	E
		D	E	L	E	T	E		O	L	M
	B		R			O	D	D			O
S	E	A		P		R		R		A	
	A	D	L	I	B		B	A	N	D	Y
B	U	D		S	T	A	R	G	A	Z	E
		S	H	A	W		A	S	S	E	T

No. 9

	E			E		I					
	C	A	A	N		B	U	M	P	E	R
T	O	P	S	I	D	E		A	R	M	Y
		P	H	D		R		W	I	S	E
		R			O	I	K		C		
T	H	O	U		T	A	U		K	E	I
	O	P	S		I		D	Y	L	A	N
	D	R	E	G	S		U		Y	U	M
	S	I	R	E		A			P		A
		A		M	A	N	I	F	E	S	T
O	C	T			I	N	F	L	A	M	E
	R	E	S		D	E	S	I	R	E	S
	I	N	N	S				N			
	M	E	A		C	R	I	T	I	C	S
	E	S	C	A	P	E	D		T	U	E
	A	S	K		U	F	O		V	E	T

No. 10

	O		N		R		G			M	
	B		O		E		A	H	A	B	
M	A	N	U	F	A	C	T	U	R	E	R
	M	E	N	U	S		E	R	A		A
P	A	C		N	O	D			B	M	I
		T		K	N	O	W		L	A	S
	L	A	B			M		W	E	R	E
	U	R	L		L	I	P			T	
	K	I	A		E	N	A		D	I	E
T	E	N	S		N	A	G		A	N	N
		E	T	H	A	N	E		B	I	D
	C		S			C	R	U			S
N	U	B		B		E		S		B	
	B	L	E	E	D		J	U	D	A	S
S	A	O		D	E	M	E	R	A	R	A
		C	L	E	F		T	Y	P	E	S

No. 11

				S		A			F		
T	R	A	C	T	O	R			L	A	D
	O	A	H	U		M	A	D	A	M	E
S	T	A	I	D			F		G	A	P
	A		M	I	D	S	T				A
	T		N	O	O	K		N	O	I	R
W	I	N	E		R	A	W		M	O	T
	O		Y				E		G	U	M
D	N	A		B	L	A	B				E
		G		R	A	M		J	O	H	N
B	A	R		E	P	E	E		P	U	T
	M	E	O	W		N	Y	M	P	H	S
B	Y	E			U	A	E		R		
		I	D	S		B		S	E	C	S
		N	E	P	A	L		A	S	H	E
R	U	G	B	Y		E	D	I	S	O	N

No. 12

	B						H		C		
	U	P	S	E	T		E	S	H	E	R
	R	E	P	L	I	C	A	T	E		O
	G	L	O	B	E		D	R	A	M	A
	L	I	R	A		C		U	P	O	N
	A	C	T		H	O	S	T	E	L	
	R	A	Y	S		L			S	A	D
F	A	N			S	U	M	A	T	R	A
	L		R		M	M	E				Z
	A	S	P		E	N	S	N	A	R	E
	R	U	M		E	S	S	A	Y	E	D
A	M	P						V	E	E	
		P	E	A	C	H		E			A
	B	O	X	W	O	O	D		B	S	C
		R	E	A	L	L	Y		L	A	M
G	U	T	S	Y		D	E	L	U	X	E

No. 13

				W		M				M	
Z	E	B	R	A		O	R	A	T	O	R
	N	O	O	D	L	E		P	H	D	
	N	O	W					P	E	E	R
	U			T	A	J		L	I	M	A
T	I	D	A	L	W	A	V	E	S		N
		O		C	E	P		S	T	A	G
R	O	Z			S	A	T			G	
	R	E	M			N		G	A	R	B
O	B	S	E	R	V	E	R		L	E	E
	S		T	E	A	S	E		P	E	N
			E	S	S	E	X		H		
P	E	G		P				L	A	M	A
	M	A	L	I	G	N	S		B	O	N
G	I	G		R	E	G	I	M	E	N	T
	T		V	E	N	O	M		T	O	S

No. 14

	C						S		P		
	O	P	T	E	D		P	E	R	O	N
	N	A	R	R	A	T	I	V	E		O
	G	R	A	I	N		T	I	D	E	S
	R	A	C	E		E		C	I	T	Y
	A	P	E		C	L	U	T	C	H	
	T	E	S	T		E			T	O	M
P	U	T			I	M	P	A	S	S	E
	L		O		K	E	A				T
	A	P	R		E	N	T	I	T	L	E
	T	E	G		A	T	E	L	I	E	R
P	E	R						L	A	X	
		S	L	A	B	S		S			H
	D	I	A	R	I	E	S		F	R	Y
		S	T	I	T	C	H		B	U	D
S	A	T	E	D		S	H	R	I	N	E

No. 15

			U				O		L		
S	H	U	N		R		F	R	A	N	C
	I	N	F	L	E	C	T		V	A	L
R	E	C	O	I	L			B	A	N	A
		O	L	D	E	S	T				N
	W	M	D		N	E	W		S	I	D
		M			T	A	I		O	D	E
G	L	U	G		S	T	R	I	P	E	S
	A	N	Y				L				T
	R	I	P	P	E	D		G	E	R	I
V	A	C		U	M	A		A	V	O	N
		A	N	N	I	H	I	L	A	T	E
		T				L					
B	L	I	M	P	S		S	H	U	T	S
	E	V	A	D	E		K	A	Z	O	O
	D	E	I	F	I	C	A	T	I	O	N

No. 16

				S		S				B	
S	T	A	G	E		O	R	I	O	L	E
	A	B	A	C	U	S		D	R	U	
	N	U	T					L	A	N	D
	G			M	B	A		I	N	T	O
C	O	M	P	E	L	L	I	N	G		O
		E		T	O	T		G	E	R	M
B	E	D			W	E	D			E	
	T	I	T			R		M	A	C	E
O	C	C	U	P	I	E	R		C	U	L
	H		B	I	N	G	E		A	R	F
			A	R	S	O	N		D		
B	Y	E		A				D	E	C	O
	A	M	E	N	D	E	D		M	A	R
S	M	S		H	I	L	A	R	I	T	Y
	S		R	A	N	K	S		C	O	X

No. 17

				B		H			S		
B	A	P	T	I	S	M			L	E	S
	P	U	R	L		M	O	T	I	V	E
K	E	B	A	B			I		D	E	L
	R		C	A	B	A	L				F
	T		T	O	I	L		P	E	L	E
E	U	R	O		O	F	F		L	E	V
	R		R				A		M	O	I
K	E	G		C	R	I	B				D
		A		H	I	D		R	U	S	E
Z	Z	Z		I	B	I	S		P	A	N
	O	P	E	N		O	U	T	F	I	T
B	E	A			A	L	B		R		
		C	G	I		E		L	O	S	S
		H	A	V	O	C		A	N	K	A
M	O	O	D	Y		T	A	C	T	I	C

No. 18

			S				M		F		
C	R	O	C		F		A	L	O	F	T
	I	N	H	A	L	E	D		O	A	R
P	A	C	I	F	Y			E	T	T	A
		E	S	T	H	E	R				M
	D	I	M		A	V	E		U	S	P
		N			L	I	L		R	H	O
S	T	A	R		F	L	A	N	N	E	L
	O	B	I				X				I
	G	L	O	W	E	R		E	L	A	N
Y	O	U		A	W	E		L	O	W	E
		E	S	S	E	N	T	I	A	L	S
		M				D					
P	O	O	D	L	E		A	R	O	M	A
	L	O	S	E	R		R	A	R	E	R
	E	N	L	A	R	G	E	M	E	N	T

No. 19

			I					B		E	
U	D	O	N		D	A	R	E		Q	
	I	N	C	R	E	D	U	L	O	U	S
	S	T	U		V	A	S		B	I	N
	C	A	R	D	I		T	E	S	L	A
T	O	P			L	O	L		T	A	P
	V		D				E	X	I	T	
	E	M	I	N	E	M			N	E	E
	R	E	M	O	V	E		C	A	R	P
	E	N	S	N	A	R	E		T	A	I
D	R	U		E		G			E	L	S
			W		S	E	T	S			C
	F	I	T		T		O		O	N	O
	L	O	O	F	A	H	S		P	I	P
R	O	N		I	R	A		H	E	R	A
		A	L	B	E	D	O		C	O	L

No. 20

				P		D				M	
R	I	O	J	A		I	N	D	I	A	N
	S	L	A	T	E	D		E	S	C	
	A	M	Y					C	O	R	D
	A			G	O	T		E	B	O	R
A	C	R	O	P	H	O	B	I	A		O
		U		S	I	P		T	R	A	P
G	R	R			O	O	H			L	
	O	A	F			L		I	S	P	Y
L	O	L	L	I	P	O	P		T	H	E
	F		A	M	I	G	O		R	A	N
			K	A	N	Y	E		E		
V	O	W		G				P	A	R	R
	O	R	D	I	N	A	L		M	O	O
S	P	Y		N	O	T	E	L	E	S	S
	S		S	E	V	E	N		R	E	S

No. 21

			C					L		S	
A	V	E	R		F	L	U	E		P	
	A	M	E	L	I	O	R	A	T	E	S
	M	A	P		E	B	B		A	C	E
	P	I	T	O	N		A	O	R	T	A
N	I	L			D	U	N		D	A	N
	R		Z				E	R	I	C	
	E	L	I	S	H	A			N	U	T
	B	A	N	T	A	M		R	E	L	Y
	A	N	G	E	L	I	C		S	A	P
U	T	E		T		N			S	R	I
			L		M	O	S	S			C
	P	H	I		E		H		E	N	A
	R	E	P	U	L	S	E		M	E	L
C	O	R		P	E	A		D	I	A	L
		B	E	S	E	T	S		T	R	Y

No. 22

	B		C		R		V			B	
	U		U		U		O	B	E	Y	
O	L	D	F	A	S	H	I	O	N	E	D
	B	E	F	I	T		D	A	M		I
D	S	T		L	I	V			I	T	V
		A		S	C	A	N		T	E	A
	T	I	M			L		G	Y	M	S
	A	N	I		S	U	N			P	
	K	I	D		L	E	T		P	E	G
F	E	N	D		A	L	I		U	R	N
		G	L	U	T	E	N		B	A	A
	P		E			S	I	M			W
H	I	P		N		S		E		L	
	C	O	C	O	A		D	A	T	U	M
L	A	M		U	N	D	U	L	A	T	E
		P	O	N	Y		A	S	P	E	N

No. 23

				J		F				S	
C	A	B	L	E		A	I	R	B	A	G
	M	O	U	T	H	Y		H	E	T	
	P	Y	X					E	W	E	S
	L			V	A	L		B	A	S	E
P	E	R	C	O	L	A	T	O	R		L
		A		W	A	D		K	E	E	L
M	A	D			N	Y	X			L	
	B	A	T			L		E	P	I	C
T	E	R	R	I	F	I	C		U	Z	I
	T		O	S	A	K	A		B	A	D
			T	O	N	E	R		L		
T	O	M		T				T	I	C	S
	R	I	P	O	S	T	E		C	O	W
L	E	X		P	A	N	O	R	A	M	A
	S		V	E	N	T	S		N	A	T

No. 24

	P			F		C					
	T	U	T	U		A	B	A	T	E	S
B	A	N	A	N	A	S		T	E	L	L
		D	U	D		I		E	M	M	Y
		E			A	N	T		P		
T	O	R	O		S	O	O		E	Y	E
	A	T	M		H		W	I	R	E	R
	T	H	A	N	E		S		A	S	A
	H	E	R	O		R			T		S
		W		R	E	A	S	S	U	R	E
U	A	E			S	C	O	U	R	E	R
	S	A	C		C	Y	P	R	E	S	S
	S	T	O	P				G			
	O	H	M		P	R	E	E	N	E	D
	R	E	F	R	A	I	N		A	V	E
	T	R	Y		T	O	D		G	E	N

No. 25

	S						A		W		
	U	R	G	E	D		L	E	A	S	T
	P	E	R	M	A	N	E	N	T		O
	E	Q	U	I	P		C	A	C	H	E
	R	U	N	T		L		C	H	A	D
	M	I	G		K	I	T	T	E	N	
	A	R	E	A		N			R	O	B
D	R	E			U	T	E	N	S	I	L
	K		Y		R	E	M				U
	E	V	A		S	L	U	M	B	E	R
	T	I	P		A	S	S	A	I	L	S
A	S	S						I	N	K	
		C	R	O	S	S		L			N
	T	O	U	G	H	E	N		A	A	A
		S	E	L	E	N	E		L	I	P
S	U	E	D	E		T	E	M	P	L	E

No. 26

				C		A			T		
A	S	H	T	R	A	Y			R	A	P
	P	E	R	U		E	Q	U	I	N	E
F	I	X	E	S			U		O	C	R
	L		M	O	C	H	A				S
	L		B	E	A	U		L	I	D	O
G	I	R	L		P	H	D		N	U	N
	N		E				I		S	E	A
K	G	B		S	M	O	G				L
		R		A	O	B		M	I	D	I
C	P	U		L	I	S	P		N	U	T
	A	N	N	E		C	R	A	G	G	Y
M	M	E			B	U	Y		R		
		T	A	B		R		D	E	F	T
		T	W	I	C	E		O	S	L	O
S	C	E	N	T		D	A	M	S	O	N

No. 27

	P		S		T		M			B	
	H		T		I		A	L	O	E	
D	O	M	E	S	T	I	C	A	L	L	Y
	T	O	T	A	L		H	O	D		A
S	O	U		L	E	E			B	T	W
		S		T	S	A	R		O	W	N
	S	E	T			G		E	Y	E	S
	P	T	O		P	E	A			A	
	A	R	T		O	R	B		S	K	A
B	R	A	T		O	N	O		R	E	X
		P	E	E	L	E	D		I	D	E
	D		R			S	E	N			D
I	R	K		T		S		E		Z	
	N	I	C	H	E		R	I	S	E	N
Z	O	E		O	B	L	I	G	A	T	E
		V	E	R	B		A	H	E	A	D

No. 28

				P		R				U	
M	A	Y	B	E		Y	E	A	R	N	S
	L	O	U	N	G	E		R	E	F	
	P	U	D					E	M	I	R
	H			F	A	B		N	O	T	E
V	A	M	P	I	R	E	B	A	T		A
		I		B	I	G		S	E	A	M
V	A	N			A	R	F			G	
	C	O	P			U		E	A	R	S
T	H	R	E	N	O	D	Y		M	E	H
	E		G	A	U	G	E		B	E	Y
			S	T	R	E	W		R		
A	C	T		A				H	O	P	S
	H	A	L	L	W	A	Y		S	A	T
F	U	G		I	M	M	U	N	I	S	E
	M		B	E	D	I	M		A	S	P

No. 29

			D					O		B	
E	C	H	O		U	S	E	D		E	
	O	U	T	S	T	A	N	D	I	N	G
	M	M	E		T	I	C		S	E	O
	P	I	S	T	E		A	B	O	V	E
T	E	D			R	U	G		L	O	S
	N		N				E	L	A	L	
	S	T	E	P	U	P			T	E	E
	A	R	I	A	N	A		T	I	N	A
	T	I	L	T	I	N	G		O	C	R
R	E	P		H		D			N	E	T
			E		P	A	L	L			H
	G	U	T		E		A		A	I	L
	A	R	C	H	E	R	S		M	A	I
I	S	A		O	V	A		S	I	G	N
		L	E	G	E	N	D		D	O	G

No. 30

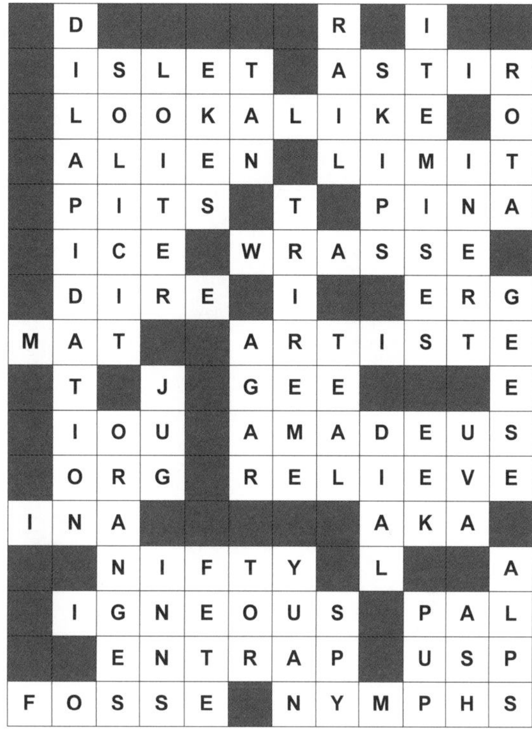

	D						R		I		
	I	S	L	E	T		A	S	T	I	R
	L	O	O	K	A	L	I	K	E		O
	A	L	I	E	N		L	I	M	I	T
	P	I	T	S		T		P	I	N	A
	I	C	E		W	R	A	S	S	E	
	D	I	R	E		I			E	R	G
M	A	T			A	R	T	I	S	T	E
	T		J		G	E	E				E
	I	O	U		A	M	A	D	E	U	S
	O	R	G		R	E	L	I	E	V	E
I	N	A						A	K	A	
		N	I	F	T	Y		L			A
	I	G	N	E	O	U	S		P	A	L
		E	N	T	R	A	P		U	S	P
F	O	S	S	E		N	Y	M	P	H	S

No. 31

	H		W		M		A			H	
	Y		E		E		S	A	G	E	
T	E	M	P	E	R	A	T	U	R	E	S
	N	A	T	A	L		I	K	E		A
P	A	C		S	I	A			E	L	S
		R		E	N	D	S		C	O	S
	D	O	S			J		L	E	V	Y
	O	C	T		T	E	L			A	
	D	O	R		E	C	O		A	B	S
N	O	S	E		S	T	U		A	L	E
		M	A	N	T	I	S		H	E	W
	S		M			V	E	G			S
H	O	B		D		E		L		B	
	F	L	O	O	R		D	O	J	O	S
S	A	O		M	A	C	A	R	O	N	I
		C	H	E	F		S	Y	N	O	D

No. 32

				A		B			S		
A	D	J	U	D	G	E			P	O	R
	R	O	T	H		N	A	T	I	V	E
L	A	T	T	E			I		N	O	V
	G		E	R	R	E	D				E
	O		R	E	A	L		B	O	H	R
B	O	R	E		W	I	T		Y	O	B
	N		D				A		L	Y	E
U	S	B		T	A	C	T				R
		A		H	U	R		L	I	R	A
G	E	L		A	G	E	D		C	U	T
	A	L	A	I		S	E	R	E	N	E
H	U	G			C	C	S		C		
		A	D	D		E		B	O	A	S
		M	O	U	R	N		A	L	B	A
B	E	E	C	H		T	A	N	D	E	M

No. 33

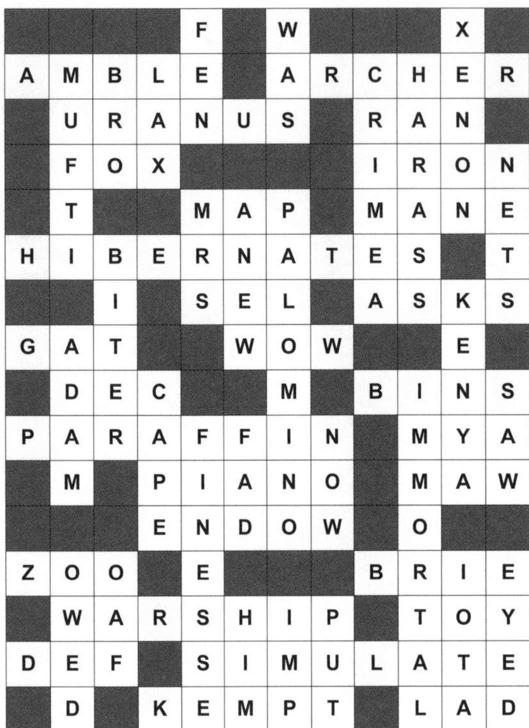

				F		W				X	
A	M	B	L	E		A	R	C	H	E	R
	U	R	A	N	U	S		R	A	N	
	F	O	X					I	R	O	N
	T			M	A	P		M	A	N	E
H	I	B	E	R	N	A	T	E	S		T
		I		S	E	L		A	S	K	S
G	A	T			W	O	W			E	
	D	E	C			M		B	I	N	S
P	A	R	A	F	F	I	N		M	Y	A
	M		P	I	A	N	O		M	A	W
			E	N	D	O	W		O		
Z	O	O		E				B	R	I	E
	W	A	R	S	H	I	P		T	O	Y
D	E	F		S	I	M	U	L	A	T	E
	D		K	E	M	P	T		L	A	D

No. 34

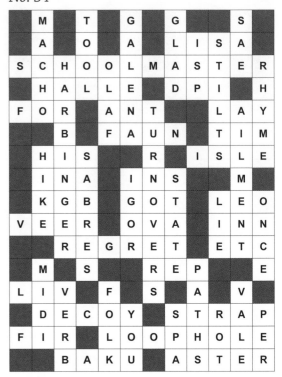

	M		T		G		G			S	
	A		O		A		L	I	S	A	
S	C	H	O	O	L	M	A	S	T	E	R
	H	A	L	L	E		D	P	I		H
F	O	R		A	N	T			L	A	Y
		B		F	A	U	N		T	I	M
	H	I	S			R		I	S	L	E
	I	N	A		I	N	S			M	
	K	G	B		G	O	T		L	E	O
V	E	E	R		O	V	A		I	N	N
		R	E	G	R	E	T		E	T	C
	M		S			R	E	P			E
L	I	V		F		S		A		V	
	D	E	C	O	Y		S	T	R	A	P
F	I	R		L	O	O	P	H	O	L	E
		B	A	K	U		A	S	T	E	R

No. 35

	D						S		D		
	I	M	A	G	O		A	B	E	T	S
	S	I	D	E	L	I	N	E	S		A
	P	L	U	M	E		K	N	O	C	K
	E	L	L	S		D		C	L	U	E
	N	I	T		M	I	S	H	A	P	
	S	O	S	O		S			T	I	C
H	A	N			T	O	R	P	E	D	O
	T		E		O	B	I				P
	I	R	A		R	E	P	U	L	S	E
	O	A	R		E	Y	E	L	E	T	S
G	N	U						N	A	Y	
		C	R	I	B	S		A			P
	W	O	O	D	R	O	W		E	G	O
		U	M	L	A	U	T		M	A	R
C	A	S	E	Y		R	O	B	U	S	T

No. 36

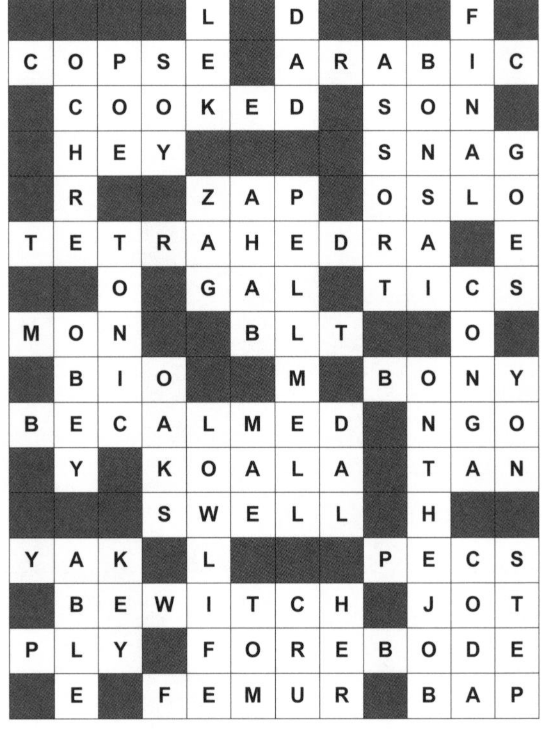

				L		D				F	
C	O	P	S	E		A	R	A	B	I	C
	C	O	O	K	E	D		S	O	N	
	H	E	Y					S	N	A	G
	R			Z	A	P		O	S	L	O
T	E	T	R	A	H	E	D	R	A		E
		O		G	A	L		T	I	C	S
M	O	N			B	L	T			O	
	B	I	O			M		B	O	N	Y
B	E	C	A	L	M	E	D		N	G	O
	Y		K	O	A	L	A		T	A	N
			S	W	E	L	L		H		
Y	A	K		L				P	E	C	S
	B	E	W	I	T	C	H		J	O	T
P	L	Y		F	O	R	E	B	O	D	E
	E		F	E	M	U	R		B	A	P

No. 37

	P		C		I		D			I	
	A		O		C		O	P	A	L	
U	N	F	A	V	O	U	R	A	B	L	E
	T	O	X	I	N		M	R	S		V
S	O	L		S	I	R			U	M	A
		L		A	C	E	S		R	A	N
	M	O	A			C		A	D	D	S
	A	W	L		T	U	M			N	
	D	E	L		O	R	A		N	E	O
M	E	R	E		O	R	G		E	S	P
		S	Y	S	T	E	M		D	S	T
	Z		S			N	A	P			S
B	E	D		C		T		I		E	
	B	R	O	O	D		W	A	R	M	S
D	U	A		P	A	R	A	N	O	I	A
		G	A	S	P		D	O	W	N	Y

No. 38

			E					O		E	
I	C	E	D		C	R	A	M		M	
	L	A	U	G	H	I	N	G	G	A	S
	O	R	C		E	G	O		U	N	A
	D	E	E	D	S		R	E	A	C	T
P	H	D			S	I	A		T	I	E
	O		B				K	E	E	P	
	P	R	O	P	E	L			M	A	C
	P	A	N	I	N	I		D	A	T	A
	E	C	O	N	O	M	Y		L	E	T
C	R	Y		A		B			A	D	A
			E		S	O	N	G			M
	J	A	N		H		H		M	Y	A
	A	R	D	U	O	U	S		O	U	R
H	M	M		R	A	F		L	O	L	A
		Y	E	L	L	O	W		T	E	N

No. 39

	C			U		T					
	A	F	A	R		I	T	S	E	L	F
S	T	O	P	G	A	P		P	A	I	L
		U	R	E		T		A	R	T	Y
		R			H	O	G		T		
R	E	D	O		E	E	L		H	U	T
	R	I	B		A		A	R	E	N	A
	A	M	O	U	R		D		N	O	B
	S	E	E	K		A			W		L
		N		E	S	C	A	P	A	D	E
O	P	S			I	N	H	E	R	I	T
	A	I	M		N	E	A	T	E	N	S
	N	O	A	H				E			
	A	N	N		O	C	A	R	I	N	A
	M	A	I	L	B	O	X		F	O	P
	A	L	A		E	R	E		S	M	E

No. 40

				H		B				D	
V	A	G	U	E		C	A	D	R	E	S
	C	O	G	N	A	C		R	E	V	
	O	O	H					I	S	I	S
	R			B	I	B		V	I	L	E
I	N	T	R	O	D	U	C	E	D		E
		H		P	E	R		N	E	O	N
P	S	I			A	G	O			C	
	H	E	M			L		S	P	E	D
L	I	F	E	S	P	A	N		R	A	Y
	N		O	C	H	R	E		O	N	E
			W	R	I	S	T		L		
P	E	P		A				L	I	M	A
	L	O	U	T	I	S	H		F	O	R
A	M	P		C	R	E	E	P	I	N	G
	S		C	H	E	W	Y		C	O	O

No. 41

	G		L		F		W			C	
	R		A		E		A	J	A	R	
C	I	R	R	O	S	T	R	A	T	U	S
	M	E	A	N	T		P	R	O		I
S	E	P		C	E	O			N	I	L
		U		E	R	R	S		E	M	O
	I	D	S			G		A	S	P	S
	D	I	E		M	A	I			R	
	L	A	W		A	N	D		S	O	L
Y	E	T	I		T	I	A		I	V	Y
		E	N	M	E	S	H		R	E	N
	F		G			M	O	G			X
Z	E	D		J		S		U		C	
	T	O	P	A	Z		M	E	D	A	L
H	A	D		D	E	R	I	S	O	R	Y
		O	M	E	N		A	S	H	E	N

No. 42

				D		C				L	
G	A	M	M	A		W	H	I	T	E	R
	D	I	A	D	E	M		M	U	M	
	E	C	G					A	X	O	N
	L			B	B	C		G	E	N	E
V	E	N	T	I	L	A	T	E	D		V
		I		C	U	R		S	O	M	E
D	A	N			R	O	Z			A	
	K	O	P			T		W	O	N	T
F	I	N	I	S	H	E	D		N	T	H
	N		S	A	U	N	A		T	A	Y
			A	B	B	E	Y		H		
D	A	B		B				G	E	L	S
	C	U	R	A	B	L	E		J	I	M
L	E	N		T	O	I	L	S	O	M	E
	D		G	H	O	U	L		B	O	W

No. 43

			S				L		K		
C	R	O	P		A		E	V	I	T	A
	E	N	A	B	L	E	D		W	I	G
S	A	C	R	U	M			P	I	E	R
		E	S	S	A	Y	S				I
	H	I	E		N	O	H		A	R	C
		N			A	G	A		L	O	U
S	C	A	B		C	A	P	I	T	O	L
	A	B	I				E				T
	F	L	O	O	R	S		B	A	K	U
L	E	U		R	O	E		A	M	I	R
		E	L	E	C	T	O	R	A	T	E
		M				T					
A	B	O	A	R	D		L	E	N	D	S
	M	O	V	I	E		A	R	I	A	S
	I	N	A	D	V	I	S	A	B	L	E

No. 44

	C						V		R		
	O	R	D	E	R		A	F	O	O	T
	N	E	R	V	O	U	S	L	Y		E
	S	P	E	E	D		T	I	A	R	A
	E	L	A	N		C		P	L	U	M
	R	I	M		F	O	S	S	I	L	
	V	E	T	S		N			S	E	C
T	A	D			S	C	E	P	T	R	E
	T		P		C	I	A				N
	O	V	A		A	S	S	A	U	L	T
	R	E	P		R	E	T	I	N	A	S
A	Y	R						D	I	P	
		T	O	G	A	S		E			A
	M	I	R	A	G	E	S		P	A	X
		G	A	T	E	A	U		O	W	L
W	H	O	L	E		S	E	T	T	E	E

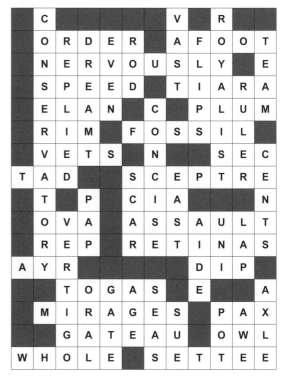

No. 45

				G		I				Y	
O	S	C	A	R		S	L	O	P	E	D
	T	H	R	U	S	H		R	A	M	
	O	I	K					A	P	E	S
	M			S	M	S		L	A	N	K
C	A	U	T	I	O	U	S	L	Y		Y
		R		S	O	S		Y	A	L	E
G	I	G			D	P	I			E	
	B	E	E			E		P	R	O	M
M	I	S	S	P	E	N	D		E	N	A
	S		P	R	I	S	E		P	A	N
			Y	O	D	E	L		R		
F	B	I		M				D	I	V	A
	A	C	C	O	U	N	T		S	A	I
P	L	Y		T	H	O	U	S	A	N	D
	E		G	E	T	U	P		L	E	S

No. 46

	D		T		R		S			W	
	R		A		E		E	P	E	E	
F	I	E	L	D	G	L	A	S	S	E	S
	V	A	C	U	A		M	I	C		K
R	E	G		S	I	N			A	G	A
		L		K	N	O	T		P	I	T
	D	E	B			T		G	E	N	E
	E	E	L		L	O	P			G	
	M	Y	A		U	R	I		A	H	A
T	I	E	R		M	I	N		D	A	R
		D	E	S	P	O	T		S	M	E
	G		D			U	S	B			S
R	O	C		D		S		R		H	
	T	H	R	O	B		V	O	W	E	D
R	O	E		J	A	N	I	T	O	R	S
		F	O	O	D		C	H	E	S	T

No. 47

	C						S		S		
	O	A	S	E	S		P	U	T	O	N
	N	E	C	T	A	R	I	N	E		O
	G	R	A	N	D		N	I	E	C	E
	L	O	L	A		B		O	R	A	L
	O	B	E		T	A	N	N	I	N	
	M	I	S	O		B			N	O	M
P	E	C			C	O	L	O	G	N	E
	R		Y		H	O	E				T
	A	R	E		I	N	S	T	A	T	E
	T	I	N		A	S	S	A	Y	E	R
P	E	P						P	E	N	
		E	L	A	N	D		S			P
	K	N	O	W	H	O	W		D	Z	O
		E	R	A	S	E	R		I	O	N
B	U	D	D	Y		S	Y	D	N	E	Y

No. 48

			I					G		A	
S	P	A	R		L	O	N	E		B	
	E	L	A	B	O	R	A	T	I	O	N
	N	O	T		O	A	T		N	M	E
	C	H	E	E	P		U	N	T	I	E
M	I	A			S	L	R		E	N	D
	L		T				E	Z	R	A	
	C	E	A	S	E	D			S	T	U
	A	C	C	U	S	E		V	E	I	N
	S	H	O	R	T	L	Y		C	O	E
N	E	O		F		T			T	N	T
			R		L	A	D	S			H
	A	B	E		E		O		A	N	I
	D	E	P	L	O	Y	S		T	I	C
B	A	A		O	N	O		I	O	N	A
		T	R	U	A	N	T		P	A	L

No. 49

				Z		C				A	
B	O	C	C	E		A	L	A	R	M	S
	T	A	W	D	R	Y		C	A	B	
	H	M	M					O	V	I	D
	E			S	A	S		R	A	T	E
P	R	O	T	E	C	T	I	N	G		A
		O		A	I	R		S	E	R	F
F	E	Z			D	I	M			I	
	R	E	D			K		D	I	S	C
E	N	D	A	N	G	E	R		M	E	G
	E		C	A	I	R	O		P	S	I
			E	R	A	S	E		R		
W	I	G		R				G	O	T	O
	B	A	H	A	M	A	S		V	I	A
T	E	D		T	A	S	H	K	E	N	T
	X		D	E	C	A	Y		D	E	S

No. 50

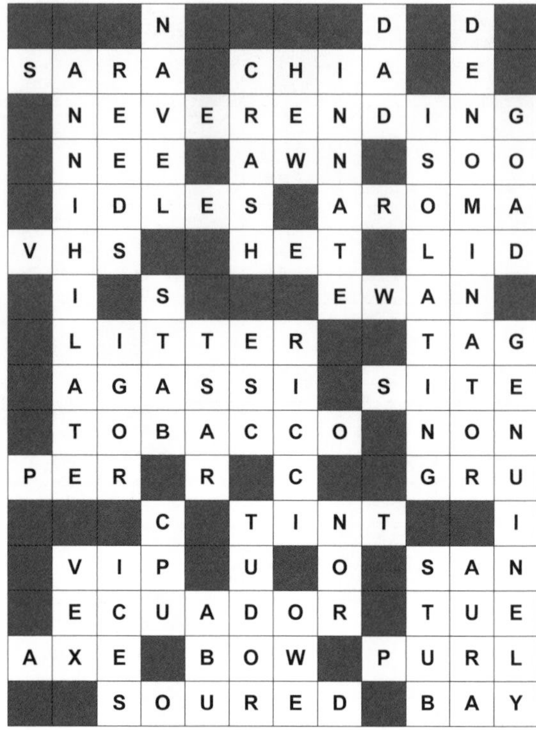

N D D
S A R A C H I A E
N E V E R E N D I N G
N E E A W N S O O
I D L E S A R O M A
V H S H E T L I D
I S E W A N
L I T T E R T A G
A G A S S I S I T E
T O B A C C O N O N
P E R R C G R U
C T I N T I
V I P U O S A N
E C U A D O R T U E
A X E B O W P U R L
S O U R E D B A Y

No. 51

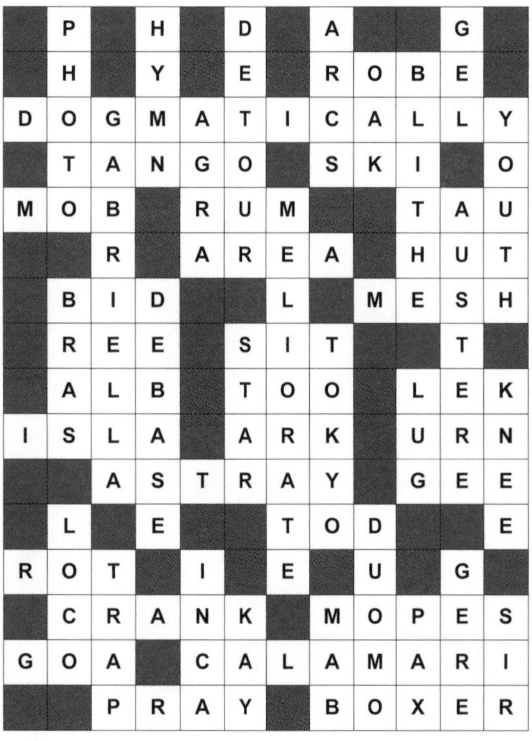

No. 52

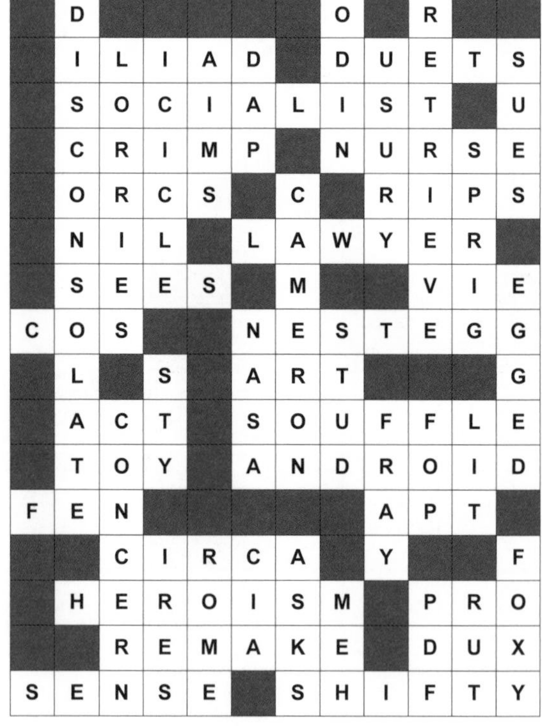

No. 53

				G		S				A	
B	A	S	T	E		A	R	A	B	L	E
	B	I	O	T	I	C		B	R	O	
	O	P	T					I	O	N	S
	U			T	A	J		D	O	G	E
S	T	I	P	U	L	A	T	E	D		N
		O		P	U	P		D	Y	A	D
D	E	N			M	A	T			R	
	M	I	R			N		V	E	R	A
C	U	C	U	M	B	E	R		L	A	W
	S		L	A	P	S	E		L	Y	N
			E	S	S	E	X		I		
J	A	B		C				E	P	P	S
	S	C	R	A	W	L	S		S	E	I
M	I	C		R	O	Y	A	L	I	S	T
	A		W	A	K	E	N		S	O	S

No. 54

	C			U		I					
	H	O	G	S		S	T	A	B	L	E
D	I	N	N	E	R	S		R	O	O	K
		C	U	D		U		F	U	S	E
		E			R	E	M		R		
F	L	I	P		O	D	E		G	Y	P
	A	N	A		W		S	W	E	A	R
	R	A	I	D	S		H		O	W	E
	A	B	L	Y		G			I		T
		L		E	V	A	N	E	S	C	E
B	L	U			E	L	U	S	I	O	N
	E	E	L		E	A	S	T	E	N	D
	A	M	O	K				E			
	N	O	U		P	U	E	R	I	L	E
	T	O	S	S	I	N	G		S	I	C
	O	N	E		G	I	G		A	L	U

No. 55

			P					F		E	
A	F	A	R		P	E	R	U		X	
	U	T	I	L	I	T	A	R	I	A	N
	T	O	N		L	A	B		N	M	E
	U	L	T	R	A		B	A	S	I	C
U	R	L			U	R	I		I	N	K
	I		C				T	I	N	A	
	S	T	U	C	C	O			U	T	C
	T	E	T	H	E	R		P	A	I	R
	I	N	S	I	P	I	D		T	O	E
A	C	T		P		B			E	N	D
			S		M	I	T	E			U
	U	S	A		O		I		P	O	L
	S	T	O	P	G	A	P		A	H	I
A	B	E		A	U	G		U	N	I	T
		M	E	D	L	E	Y		T	O	Y

No. 56

			S				E		S		
D	E	F	T		S		E	N	T	E	R
	R	O	E	B	U	C	K		A	A	H
P	A	U	P	E	R			I	N	T	O
		R	U	E	F	U	L				D
	G	D	P		A	P	U		M	M	E
		I			C	O	R		O	B	I
M	A	M	A		E	N	E	M	I	E	S
	N	E	W				S				L
	K	N	E	A	D	S		A	R	I	A
G	A	S		L	I	U		D	A	R	N
		I	N	T	E	R	E	S	T	E	D
		O				F					
C	A	N	A	D	A		G	L	A	D	E
	L	A	G	E	R		R	A	R	E	R
	B	L	O	C	K	B	U	S	T	E	R

No. 57

				B		T				L	
S	C	U	B	A		W	A	L	K	E	D
	A	K	I	M	B	O		A	I	M	
	P	E	G					S	M	U	G
	R			B	A	G		T	O	R	I
W	I	N	D	S	C	R	E	E	N		L
		Y		T	E	E		D	O	H	A
O	W	L			D	E	W			A	
	O	O	H			N		N	I	N	A
V	A	N	I	S	H	E	S		N	O	B
	D		S	N	A	R	L		T	I	C
			S	A	T	Y	R		R		
H	I	D		P				Y	E	T	I
	D	E	S	P	A	I	R		P	U	G
E	L	F		E	X	C	U	S	I	N	G
	E		G	R	E	E	T		D	A	Y

No. 58

	C						A		N		
	O	R	G	A	N		L	E	O	N	A
	N	E	E	D	I	N	E	S	S		I
	S	C	O	O	T		S	H	E	A	R
	E	R	R	S		H		E	D	D	Y
	R	U	G		H	Y	B	R	I	D	
	V	I	E	W		D			V	O	X
C	A	T			P	R	O	G	E	N	Y
	T		N		L	A	M				L
	I	C	Y		U	N	A	W	A	R	E
	S	O	X		S	T	R	A	T	U	M
E	M	U						R	E	N	
		P	S	A	L	M		E			R
	F	L	A	R	E	U	P		Y	A	Y
		E	N	I	G	M	A		A	V	A
C	A	S	E	D		S	P	O	K	E	N

No. 59

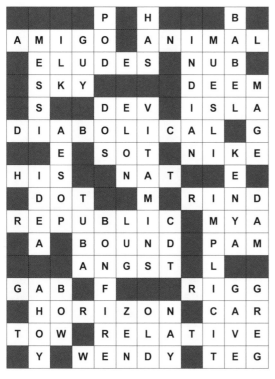

				P		H				B	
A	M	I	G	O		A	N	I	M	A	L
	E	L	U	D	E	S		N	U	B	
	S	K	Y					D	E	E	M
	S			D	E	V		I	S	L	A
D	I	A	B	O	L	I	C	A	L		G
		E		S	O	T		N	I	K	E
H	I	S			N	A	T			E	
	D	O	T			M		R	I	N	D
R	E	P	U	B	L	I	C		M	Y	A
	A		B	O	U	N	D		P	A	M
			A	N	G	S	T		L		
G	A	B		F				R	I	G	G
	H	O	R	I	Z	O	N		C	A	R
T	O	W		R	E	L	A	T	I	V	E
	Y		W	E	N	D	Y		T	E	G

No. 60

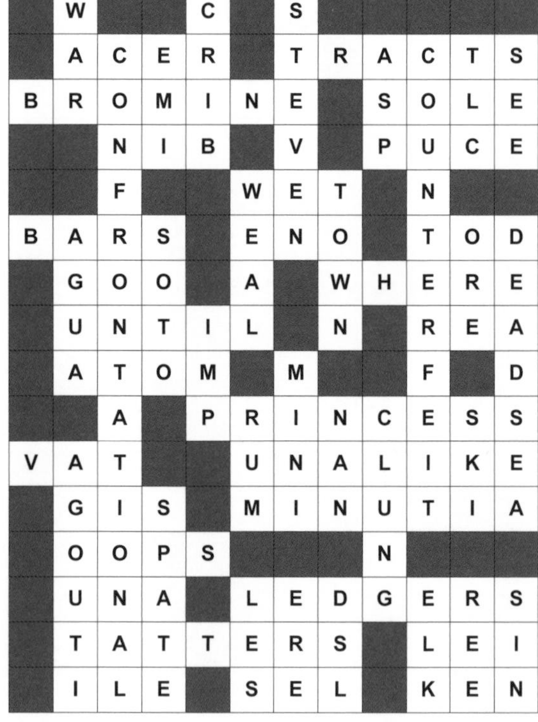

	W			C		S					
	A	C	E	R		T	R	A	C	T	S
B	R	O	M	I	N	E		S	O	L	E
		N	I	B		V		P	U	C	E
		F			W	E	T		N		
B	A	R	S		E	N	O		T	O	D
	G	O	O		A		W	H	E	R	E
	U	N	T	I	L		N		R	E	A
	A	T	O	M		M			F		D
		A		P	R	I	N	C	E	S	S
V	A	T			U	N	A	L	I	K	E
	G	I	S		M	I	N	U	T	I	A
	O	O	P	S				N			
	U	N	A		L	E	D	G	E	R	S
	T	A	T	T	E	R	S		L	E	I
	I	L	E		S	E	L		K	E	N

No. 61

			A					I		O	
A	G	E	S		R	H	E	A		M	
	O	N	C	L	O	U	D	N	I	N	E
	O	V	O		A	B	I		M	I	N
	D	O	T	E	S		T	E	M	P	T
A	N	Y			T	I	E		E	O	S
	E		C				D	I	R	T	
	S	L	O	P	E	S			S	E	W
	S	I	E	R	R	A		V	I	N	E
	M	A	N	A	G	U	A		O	C	A
H	E	M		M		C			N	E	T
			A		S	E	L	L			H
	A	M	P		K		O		A	L	E
	H	A	R	P	I	S	T		J	A	R
T	A	R		P	E	T		S	A	L	E
		C	H	E	R	Y	L		R	A	D

No. 62

				B		E				S	
K	A	F	K	A		S	A	U	N	A	S
	P	O	E	T	I	C		R	I	B	
	R	E	G					A	C	R	E
	O			H	A	N		N	E	E	D
I	N	G	L	O	R	I	O	U	S		G
		H		W	A	N		S	T	A	Y
Q	U	O			B	E	T			U	
	S	U	P			T		D	A	D	S
R	E	L	E	A	S	E	D		P	I	E
	S		G	R	E	E	R		P	O	P
			S	T	O	N	Y		R		
V	H	S		D				Y	O	L	K
	E	A	S	E	O	F	F		V	A	N
P	E	W		C	A	R	O	T	E	N	E
	D		T	O	K	Y	O		D	A	W

No. 63

			M				E		J		
R	A	T	E		F		C	H	A	R	D
	S	H	A	K	I	N	G		P	A	R
T	A	R	G	E	T			S	E	G	A
		O	R	A	T	O	R				W
	A	W	E		E	M	O		C	D	T
		I			S	A	P		I	S	H
I	O	N	A		T	R	E	A	D	L	E
	A	T	M				S				L
	T	H	Y	M	U	S		M	I	D	I
C	H	E		A	S	P		B	O	O	N
		T	U	R	B	U	L	E	N	C	E
		O				R					
U	P	W	A	R	D		S	P	L	A	Y
	E	E	R	I	E		R	A	I	S	E
	C	L	E	A	N	L	I	N	E	S	S

No. 64

	C		A		P		Y			W	
	A		C		I		E	S	P	Y	
N	I	G	H	T	C	L	O	T	H	E	S
	R	A	Y	O	N		H	U	R		O
F	O	R		D	I	P			A	W	L
		G		O	C	H	E		S	E	I
	C	O	G			Y		S	E	E	D
	O	Y	L		A	S	K			V	
	P	L	Y		K	I	A		E	I	D
D	E	E	P		I	C	Y		A	L	I
		S	H	A	N	I	A		U	S	E
	B		S			A	K	A			M
T	E	A		B		N		U		M	
	A	D	I	E	U		I	N	N	E	R
D	U	D		A	P	E	R	T	U	R	E
		S	O	N	S		E	S	S	E	X

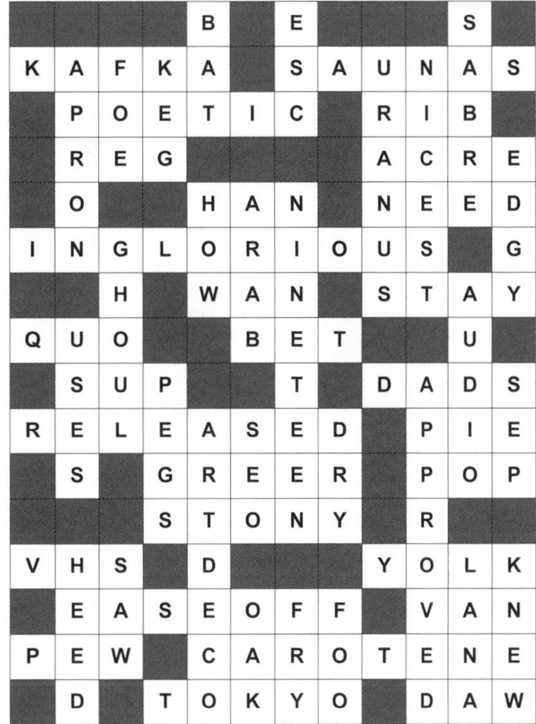

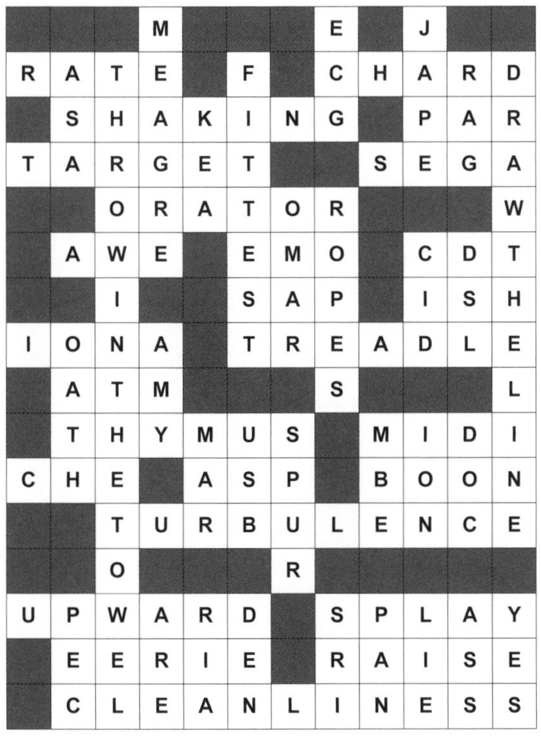

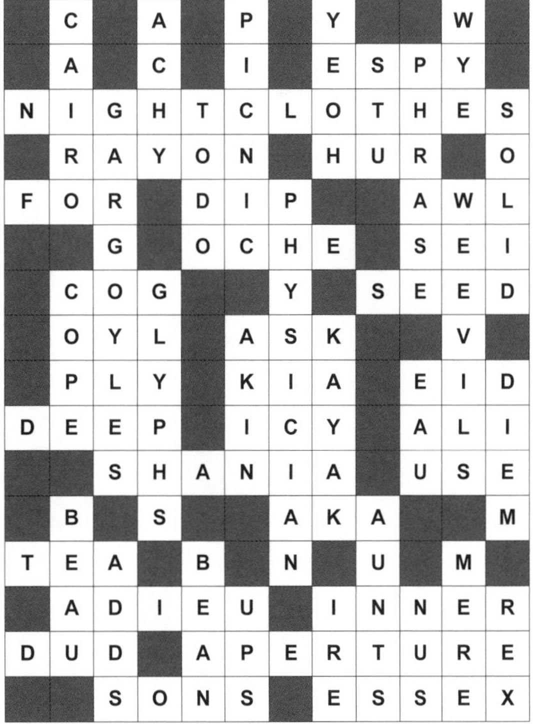

No. 65

	R						A		S		
	E	R	O	D	E		A	S	K	E	D
	D	E	N	I	G	R	A	T	E		I
	I	C	I	N	G		S	A	L	S	A
	S	L	O	E		F		Y	E	L	L
	T	A	N		F	I	E	S	T	A	
	R	I	S	E		T			O	P	T
K	I	M			I	M	M	E	N	S	E
	B		R		R	E	A				R
	U	F	O		E	N	G	U	L	F	S
	T	O	D		S	T	E	R	I	L	E
H	E	R						D	Z	O	
		C	R	I	E	R		U			I
	T	E	A	R	O	O	M		F	A	D
		P	R	O	N	T	O		O	W	L
O	L	S	E	N		A	N	Y	O	N	E

No. 66

			A				A		P		
S	T	U	N		P		C	O	U	C	H
	I	N	V	E	R	S	E		P	H	I
F	A	C	I	L	E			S	A	I	D
		O	L	I	V	E	S				E
	S	M	S		I	L	K		U	S	A
		M			E	M	I		Z	E	N
G	L	U	T		W	O	R	R	I	E	D
	A	N	N				L				S
	N	I	T	W	I	T		D	A	T	E
D	E	C		E	L	Y		O	G	L	E
		A	F	T	E	R	S	H	O	C	K
		T				O					
B	R	I	D	L	E		A	M	U	S	E
	A	V	A	I	L		H	I	R	E	R
	W	E	L	L	M	E	A	N	I	N	G

No. 67

			L					F		P	
A	P	S	O		A	B	L	E		L	
	A	C	C	O	M	P	A	N	I	E	D
	S	O	U		B	S	T		T	A	U
	S	U	S	H	I		T	H	E	S	E
V	A	T			T	E	E		R	U	T
	G		A				S	H	A	R	
	E	F	F	O	R	T			T	A	P
	W	E	A	V	E	R		V	I	B	E
	A	R	R	I	V	E	D		O	L	D
A	Y	N		D		A			N	E	E
			A		E	D	E	N			S
	C	R	Y		D		B		G	U	T
	P	E	R	T	U	R	B		O	V	A
D	U	A		I	C	Y		N	O	E	L
		R	E	P	E	A	L		N	A	S

No. 68

	D		S		J		N			O	
	I		N		I		E	B	A	Y	
U	N	F	O	R	G	I	V	A	B	L	E
	G	I	B	E	S		E	M	O		M
N	O	R		S	A	M			D	P	I
		E		T	W	E	E		E	A	T
	A	P	U			R		I	S	I	S
	B	L	T		C	C	S			N	
	B	A	T		H	I	T		I	T	V
P	A	C	E		A	L	U		F	E	E
		E	R	O	D	E	D		S	R	I
	M		S			S	Y	D			L
O	A	K		C		S		I		A	
	S	I	L	O	S		L	A	I	R	D
U	S	E		B	E	W	I	L	D	E	R
		V	I	S	A		E	S	S	A	Y

No. 69

				W		B				A	
A	I	S	L	E		C	A	T	T	L	E
	B	I	O	T	I	C		H	U	T	
	I	R	S					E	X	A	M
	Z			D	O	C		M	E	R	E
C	A	L	C	U	L	A	T	E	D		M
		I		B	A	R		S	O	H	O
M	U	M			F	A	X			A	
	D	I	G			P		W	I	N	G
M	O	T	O	R	C	A	R		N	O	U
	N		D	E	U	C	E		T	I	M
			S	P	E	E	D		R		
R	I	D		L				P	E	T	E
	D	E	B	A	U	C	H		P	U	G
C	O	N		C	H	O	O	S	I	N	G
	L		R	E	T	R	Y		D	A	Y

No. 70

				S		A			T		
G	E	N	D	E	R	S			O	U	T
	D	O	E	R		H	E	A	R	T	H
B	U	B	B	A			I		O	C	R
	C		A	P	H	I	D				E
	A		C	H	E	R		G	A	L	A
C	T	R	L		W	E	S		L	E	T
	E		E				I		I	K	E
G	D	P		E	P	P	S				N
		I		N	T	H		G	O	B	I
A	G	O		T	O	A	D		S	E	N
	O	N	E	S		N	U	T	M	E	G
M	A	E			W	T	O		O		
		E	E	K		A		A	S	T	I
		R	O	O	T	S		B	I	A	S
M	E	S	S	I		M	A	S	S	E	S

No. 71

	S		J		C		L			B	
	C		U		A		A	C	E	R	
M	U	L	T	I	L	I	N	G	U	A	L
	B	E	S	O	M		A	I	R		I
C	A	M		W	E	D			O	F	F
		O		A	D	E	N		P	U	T
	A	N	T			L		L	E	N	S
	P	S	I		S	I	C			N	
	S	O	P		U	V	A		G	I	A
P	O	L	O		M	E	N		I	L	L
		E	F	F	O	R	T		G	Y	M
	B		F			E	O	N			S
L	A	W		N		D		E		Y	
	B	E	T	A	S		A	S	S	A	Y
D	Y	E		V	O	L	A	T	I	L	E
		P	I	E	T		A	S	P	E	N

No. 72

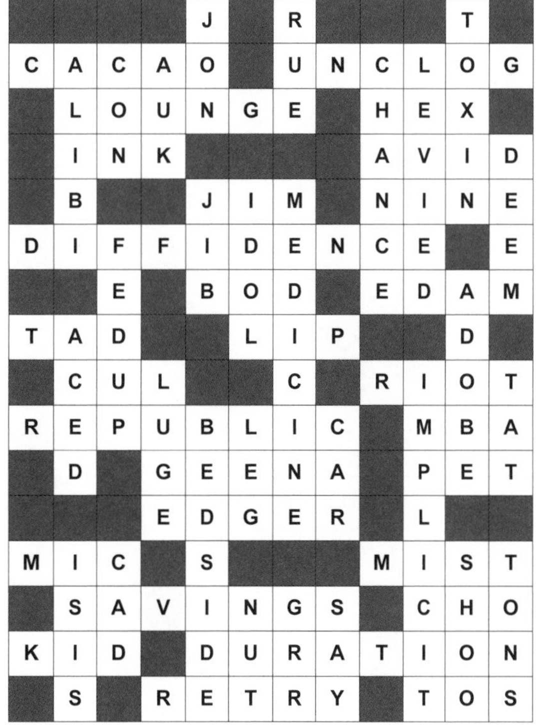

				J		R				T	
C	A	C	A	O		U	N	C	L	O	G
	L	O	U	N	G	E		H	E	X	
	I	N	K					A	V	I	D
	B			J	I	M		N	I	N	E
D	I	F	F	I	D	E	N	C	E		E
		E		B	O	D		E	D	A	M
T	A	D			L	I	P			D	
	C	U	L			C		R	I	O	T
R	E	P	U	B	L	I	C		M	B	A
	D		G	E	E	N	A		P	E	T
			E	D	G	E	R		L		
M	I	C		S				M	I	S	T
	S	A	V	I	N	G	S		C	H	O
K	I	D		D	U	R	A	T	I	O	N
	S		R	E	T	R	Y		T	O	S

No. 73

			M				F		T		
J	A	D	E		D		E	N	S	U	E
	L	I	N	S	E	E	D		A	N	N
W	A	S	T	E	S			F	R	O	G
		T	A	C	K	L	E				I
	O	I	L		T	E	L		P	U	N
		N			O	A	T		T	H	E
R	I	G	A		P	R	O	M	O	T	E
	N	U	N				N				R
	C	I	C	A	D	A		R	A	M	I
Y	E	S		Y	A	M		A	L	A	N
		H	O	R	R	I	F	Y	I	N	G
		A				D					
D	E	B	A	T	E		S	P	O	I	L
	A	L	L	O	W		S	A	U	D	I
	R	E	P	R	E	S	E	N	T	E	D

No. 74

	Z			L		C					
	I	F	F	Y		O	D	D	S	O	N
S	P	O	I	L	E	D		S	T	A	G
		U	R	E		D		T	O	R	O
		R			F	L	O		M		
A	D	D	S		L	E	U		A	P	P
	R	I	P		O		C	O	C	O	A
	A	M	A	Z	E		H		H	I	T
	G	E	R	I		E			A		R
		N		G	A	Z	P	A	C	H	O
R	E	S			F	R	E	S	H	E	N
	S	I	S		T	A	N	K	E	R	S
	C	O	N	S				E			
	A	N	A		B	R	E	W	I	N	G
	P	A	I	N	T	E	R		V	E	E
	E	L	L		W	A	R		Y	O	N

No. 75

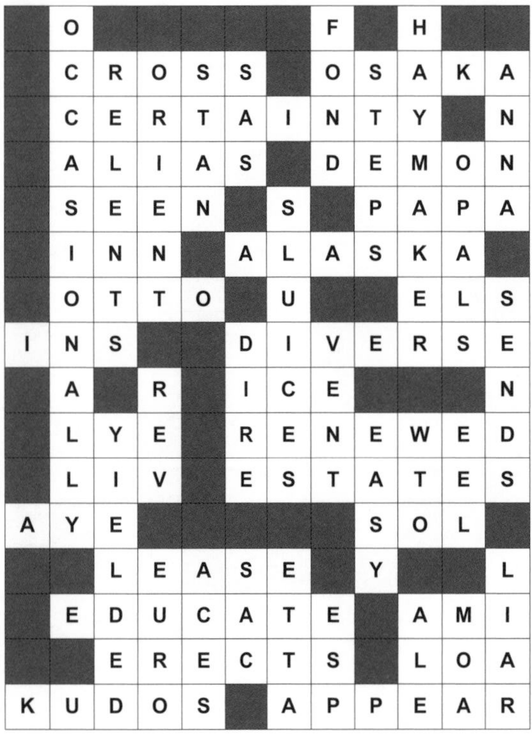

	O						F		H		
	C	R	O	S	S		O	S	A	K	A
	C	E	R	T	A	I	N	T	Y		N
	A	L	I	A	S		D	E	M	O	N
	S	E	E	N		S		P	A	P	A
	I	N	N		A	L	A	S	K	A	
	O	T	T	O		U			E	L	S
I	N	S			D	I	V	E	R	S	E
	A		R		I	C	E				N
	L	Y	E		R	E	N	E	W	E	D
	L	I	V		E	S	T	A	T	E	S
A	Y	E						S	O	L	
		L	E	A	S	E		Y			L
	E	D	U	C	A	T	E		A	M	I
		E	R	E	C	T	S		L	O	A
K	U	D	O	S		A	P	P	E	A	R

No. 76

				U		E			A		
A	S	C	E	N	T	S			B	E	D
	T	A	L	C		T	H	E	L	M	A
V	O	W	E	L			A		Y	I	N
	N		G	O	D	L	Y				G
	E		A	G	U	E		M	O	D	E
M	A	I	N		N	O	T		F	U	R
	G		T				U		F	O	O
M	E	W		S	P	A	N				U
		E		K	I	N		O	W	L	S
U	N	A		U	N	I	T		H	A	L
	O	K	R	A		M	O	I	E	T	Y
O	D	E			R	A	T		T		
		N	I	X		T		D	H	O	W
		E	L	I	T	E		N	E	R	O
W	A	D	E	S		S	C	A	R	C	E

No. 77

■	■	■	T	■	■	■	■	S	■	T	■
F	A	S	O	■	S	A	R	I	■	R	■
■	C	O	N	S	T	R	I	C	T	O	R
■	H	U	E	■	R	E	G	■	R	U	E
■	I	N	D	I	A	■	G	L	E	B	E
W	E	D	■	■	W	Y	E	■	A	L	F
■	V	■	K	■	■	■	R	U	S	E	■
■	A	F	I	E	L	D	■	■	U	S	A
■	B	E	A	N	I	E	■	P	R	O	S
■	L	E	N	I	E	N	T	■	E	M	S
V	E	T	■	D	■	T	■	■	S	E	I
■	■	■	T	■	U	S	E	S	■	■	S
■	A	C	E	■	P	■	L	■	W	E	T
■	H	O	N	E	S	T	Y	■	O	C	A
T	I	T	■	R	E	E	■	J	O	H	N
■	■	S	O	R	T	E	D	■	S	O	T

No. 78

No. 79

No. 80

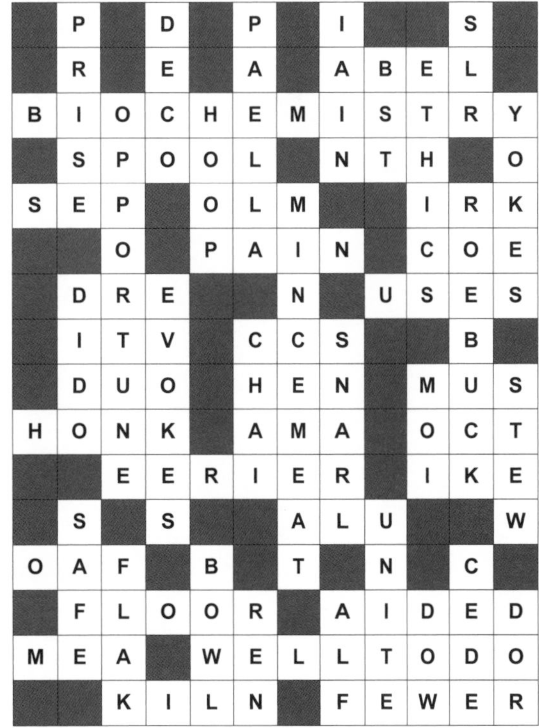

No. 81

	M						I		D		
	A	S	P	I	C		T	A	I	L	S
	S	O	A	P	O	P	E	R	A		I
	S	P	R	A	T		M	I	G	H	T
	P	R	O	D		V		S	O	U	S
	R	A	D		D	O	Z	E	N	S	
	O	N	Y	X		Y			A	K	A
I	D	O			M	A	R	I	L	Y	N
	U		J		A	G	O				D
	C	H	O		N	E	W	Y	E	A	R
	E	Y	E		E	S	S	E	N	C	E
O	D	D						T	O	E	
		R	O	A	C	H		I			T
	V	A	R	I	O	U	S		S	P	A
		T	A	R	G	E	T		O	U	R
H	E	E	L	S		S	Y	N	O	D	S

No. 82

				B		F				A	
M	A	P	L	E		E	N	I	G	M	A
	P	O	E	T	R	Y		M	A	B	
	I	L	K					P	R	I	M
	A			B	A	M		A	N	T	I
I	N	F	L	E	X	I	B	L	E		N
		I		G	I	S		A	R	I	D
Y	E	N			S	H	H			G	
	B	A	P			M		C	A	L	M
H	O	L	O	G	R	A	M		P	O	I
	R		E	R	A	S	E		E	O	N
			T	I	G	H	T		R		
J	U	L		S				T	I	L	T
	S	O	F	T	E	S	T		T	O	W
Y	E	T		L	A	K	E	S	I	D	E
	D		F	E	T	I	D		F	E	E

No. 83

				B		A			T		
P	A	R	S	L	E	Y			U	M	A
	M	I	N	I		N	I	M	B	U	S
D	E	P	O	T			R		A	D	S
	T		W	H	I	P	S				O
	H		M	E	N	U		D	I	S	C
B	Y	T	E		N	G	O		L	E	I
	S		N				A		L	O	A
U	T	E		M	I	T	T				T
		M		U	S	E		S	E	M	I
D	E	B		C	A	M	P		T	O	O
	T	A	S	K		P	I	G	E	O	N
V	A	T			D	O	E		R		
		T	A	M		R		A	N	T	E
		L	L	A	M	A		L	A	W	S
Q	U	E	U	E		L	O	L	L	O	P

No. 84

				L		D				B	
L	A	S	S	O		O	S	T	L	E	R
	N	E	I	G	H	S		H	A	T	
	V	E	X					E	V	E	S
	I			F	E	D		S	I	L	T
F	L	E	U	R	D	E	L	I	S		E
		A		Y	A	M		S	H	A	M
H	A	S			M	O	B			L	
	M	E	L			T		S	A	G	O
D	I	D	A	C	T	I	C		N	A	P
	D		Y	A	H	O	O		G	E	T
			S	P	E	N	T		L		
P	A	D		T				S	I	D	E
	T	A	R	I	F	F	S		C	A	D
H	O	W		V	A	L	I	D	A	T	E
	M		S	E	T	U	P		N	A	N

No. 85

			T					M		S	
U	P	D	O		B	A	S	E		P	
	L	I	T	H	O	S	P	H	E	R	E
	U	V	A		T	A	R		P	E	A
	R	E	L	I	C		A	R	I	A	S
D	A	D			H	E	N		C	D	T
	L		M				G	L	U	E	
	I	T	A	L	I	C			R	A	T
	S	E	N	O	R	A		L	E	G	O
	T	A	N	K	A	R	D		A	L	A
A	S	K		I		G			N	E	D
			F		P	O	M	P			S
	O	B	E		U		U		S	E	T
	W	I	Z	A	R	D	S		P	R	O
V	E	T		B	R	O		B	O	N	O
		E	L	I	S	H	A		T	E	L

No. 86

			A				A		P		
E	V	I	L		H		I	S	A	A	C
	I	N	K	W	E	L	L		P	A	L
D	E	C	A	M	P			N	A	S	A
		O	L	D	A	G	E				N
	B	M	I		T	I	A		A	D	D
		P			I	R	S		M	O	E
Y	A	R	N		C	L	E	R	I	C	S
	C	E	O				S				T
	T	H	R	E	E	S		A	S	T	I
U	S	E		L	I	T		L	O	A	N
		N	O	M	D	E	P	L	U	M	E
		S				W					
T	R	I	A	G	E		F	L	A	G	S
	Y	O	D	E	L		R	E	B	E	L
	A	N	O	N	Y	M	O	U	S	L	Y

No. 87

	B		T		A		S			S	
	L		O		N		T	R	E	E	
C	O	U	R	A	G	E	O	U	S	L	Y
	K	N	E	L	L		P	E	C		A
F	E	W		P	I	E			R	A	W
		I		S	A	N	T		O	W	N
	A	L	T			J		O	W	E	S
	F	L	Y		D	O	R			S	
	R	I	P		R	Y	E		B	O	A
T	O	N	I		A	M	A		O	M	G
		G	N	A	W	E	D		D	E	E
	C		G			N	Y	X			S
M	A	C		O		T		Y		L	
	B	L	O	C	S		C	L	O	U	T
I	S	A		H	I	T	H	E	R	T	O
		P	L	E	A		E	M	B	E	R

No. 88

				B		B				N	
G	A	M	M	A		U	S	U	R	E	R
	D	O	I	N	G	S		P	E	W	
	M	A	X					S	V	E	N
	I			V	I	A		E	I	R	E
E	X	A	C	E	R	B	A	T	E		O
		R		G	I	S		S	W	A	N
B	E	G			S	O	B			R	
	C	U	R			L		O	D	E	S
D	R	E	A	D	F	U	L		I	N	K
	U		M	E	A	T	Y		P	A	Y
			S	P	R	E	E		L		
H	A	S		L				I	O	W	A
	G	A	T	E	W	A	Y		M	I	R
H	O	G		T	Y	P	E	C	A	S	T
	G		P	E	E	P	S		S	H	Y

No. 89

	L		T		M		F			H	
	A		W		E		A	L	B	A	
A	R	T	I	S	T	I	C	A	L	L	Y
	C	A	N	O	E		T	W	O		A
V	H	S		F	O	R			U	G	H
		T		T	R	E	K		S	E	O
	D	E	S			S		P	E	S	O
	A	L	P		S	I	C			T	
	C	E	O		A	L	L		H	U	E
B	E	S	T		C	I	A		E	R	G
		S	T	A	K	E	S		M	E	G
	P		Y			N	H	S			S
Y	A	M		G		T		T		R	
	C	A	P	R	I		T	O	N	I	C
P	A	S		A	N	G	E	L	I	C	A
		H	Y	M	N		D	E	B	A	R

No. 90

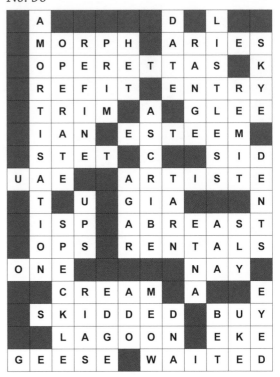

	A						D		L		
	M	O	R	P	H		A	R	I	E	S
	O	P	E	R	E	T	T	A	S		K
	R	E	F	I	T		E	N	T	R	Y
	T	R	I	M		A		G	L	E	E
	I	A	N		E	S	T	E	E	M	
	S	T	E	T		C			S	I	D
U	A	E			A	R	T	I	S	T	E
	T		U		G	I	A				N
	I	S	P		A	B	R	E	A	S	T
	O	P	S		R	E	N	T	A	L	S
O	N	E						N	A	Y	
		C	R	E	A	M		A			E
	S	K	I	D	D	E	D		B	U	Y
		L	A	G	O	O	N		E	K	E
G	E	E	S	E		W	A	I	T	E	D

No. 91

			W					E		A	
A	J	A	R		F	L	A	T		M	
	O	P	I	N	I	O	N	A	T	E	D
	U	H	T		R	U	N		A	L	A
	R	I	S	K	S		A	V	R	I	L
E	N	D			T	E	L		D	O	E
	A		E				S	T	I	R	
	L	O	L	L	O	P			N	A	T
	I	N	S	O	L	E		P	E	T	E
	S	C	A	N	D	A	L		S	E	L
N	M	E		E		R			S	S	E
			S		A	L	F	A			S
	E	C	U		R		E		L	A	C
	T	H	E	R	E	B	Y		I	D	O
E	C	O		I	N	A		H	E	A	P
		P	O	M	A	D	E		S	M	E

No. 92

				P		M				B	
L	A	P	S	E		U	N	I	S	E	X
	T	O	U	T	E	D		R	A	G	
	A	I	M					O	T	I	S
	R			J	A	R		N	I	N	E
D	I	S	C	O	V	E	R	E	R		T
		Y		B	I	N		D	E	F	T
H	A	N			D	E	V			O	
	C	O	S			G		T	A	L	K
P	E	D	E	S	T	A	L		F	I	G
	R		G	A	U	D	Y		F	O	B
			A	S	P	E	N		L		
J	A	B		H				G	I	G	I
	C	A	P	I	T	A	L		C	A	N
H	A	G		M	O	N	A	S	T	I	C
	I		W	I	N	D	Y		S	A	E

No. 93

				G		D			A		
W	E	L	C	O	M	E			L	A	D
	T	A	R	O		S	M	U	D	G	E
D	E	B	U	G			A		A	A	H
	R		S	O	U	T	H				Y
	N		A	L	G	A		S	C	U	D
H	I	N	D		H	I	E		E	A	R
	T		E				L		P	E	A
A	Y	R		E	R	I	S				T
		E		P	A	C		S	A	R	I
A	L	T		I	D	E	A		W	O	O
	E	R	I	C		C	A	N	N	O	N
V	I	A			M	R	S		I		
		C	A	Y		E		E	N	I	D
		T	H	E	T	A		O	G	R	E
P	O	S	I	T		M	I	S	S	A	L

No. 94

				F		I				N	
S	C	A	R	E		D	U	R	B	A	N
	O	S	I	E	R	S		A	I	D	
	R	H	O					S	K	I	N
	G			B	L	T		H	I	R	E
D	I	S	H	E	A	R	T	E	N		R
		T		T	O	E		R	I	C	O
C	O	O			S	A	O			A	
	W	O	N			T		L	A	R	D
E	L	L	I	P	S	I	S		P	O	E
	S		P	R	A	N	K		E	L	F
			S	O	G	G	Y		R		
T	A	J		M				M	I	S	O
	F	U	R	I	O	U	S		T	O	R
M	A	G		S	I	M	P	L	I	F	Y
	R		D	E	L	A	Y		F	A	X

No. 95

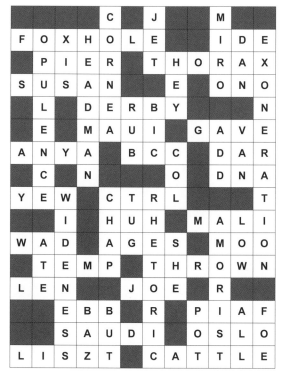

				C		J			M		
F	O	X	H	O	L	E			I	D	E
	P	I	E	R		T	H	O	R	A	X
S	U	S	A	N			E		O	N	O
	L		D	E	R	B	Y				N
	E		M	A	U	I		G	A	V	E
A	N	Y	A		B	C	C		D	A	R
	C		N				O		D	N	A
Y	E	W		C	T	R	L				T
		I		H	U	H		M	A	L	I
W	A	D		A	G	E	S		M	O	O
	T	E	M	P		T	H	R	O	W	N
L	E	N			J	O	E		R		
		E	B	B		R		P	I	A	F
		S	A	U	D	I		O	S	L	O
L	I	S	Z	T		C	A	T	T	L	E

No. 96

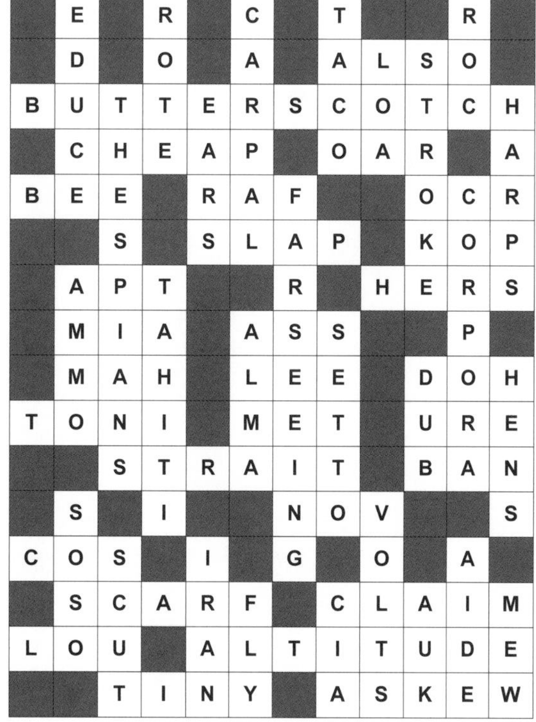

	E		R		C		T			R	
	D		O		A		A	L	S	O	
B	U	T	T	E	R	S	C	O	T	C	H
	C	H	E	A	P		O	A	R		A
B	E	E		R	A	F			O	C	R
		S		S	L	A	P		K	O	P
	A	P	T			R		H	E	R	S
	M	I	A		A	S	S			P	
	M	A	H		L	E	E		D	O	H
T	O	N	I		M	E	T		U	R	E
		S	T	R	A	I	T		B	A	N
	S		I			N	O	V			S
C	O	S		I		G		O		A	
	S	C	A	R	F		C	L	A	I	M
L	O	U		A	L	T	I	T	U	D	E
		T	I	N	Y		A	S	K	E	W

No. 97

			P				E		P		
S	K	U	A		P		F	L	O	R	A
	E	N	C	H	A	N	T		O	U	R
F	A	C	I	A	L			A	L	E	C
		O	N	W	A	R	D				H
	E	M	O		C	O	E		M	A	I
		M			E	L	L		A	P	P
S	O	U	P		S	E	T	F	R	E	E
	A	N	D				A				L
	R	I	F	F	L	E		O	K	R	A
E	S	C		B	A	D		W	I	I	G
		A	F	I	C	I	O	N	A	D	O
		T				T					
B	L	I	M	P	S		A	L	A	R	M
	E	V	E	R	Y		G	E	N	I	E
	D	E	H	Y	D	R	A	T	I	O	N

No. 98

			L					H		D	
L	A	M	A		L	U	R	E		I	
	F	O	R	G	I	V	E	N	E	S	S
	T	U	G		V	A	C		N	T	H
	E	R	O	D	E		E	X	T	R	A
U	R	N			D	A	S		R	I	M
	I		R				S	N	U	B	
	M	A	I	D	E	N			S	U	N
	A	C	C	O	S	T		O	T	T	O
	G	N	O	S	T	I	C		E	O	N
F	E	E		E		N			D	R	E
			O		S	I	P	S			N
	O	F	F		P		O		B	U	T
	R	A	T	T	L	E	R		E	L	I
C	C	S		N	A	G		C	E	N	T
		T	A	T	T	O	O		T	A	Y

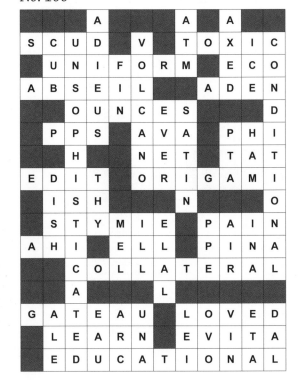

No. 99

	V			F		L					
	I	D	E	A		A	L	I	C	I	A
W	E	I	R	D	L	Y		M	O	O	N
		S	E	E		E		P	A	N	T
		T			B	R	A		G		
H	A	I	L		A	S	S		U	S	A
	G	N	U		R		I	D	L	E	R
	E	G	G	E	D		A		A	P	T
	D	U	S	T		E			T		L
		I		C	A	M	P	S	I	T	E
M	R	S			O	M	I	N	O	U	S
	O	H	M		B	Y	G	O	N	E	S
	B	A	A	S				O			
	B	B	C		U	T	O	P	I	A	N
	E	L	A	S	T	I	C		L	I	U
	D	E	W		E	N	A		E	L	S

No. 100

			A				A		A		
S	C	U	D		V		T	O	X	I	C
	U	N	I	F	O	R	M		E	C	O
A	B	S	E	I	L			A	D	E	N
		O	U	N	C	E	S				D
	P	P	S		A	V	A		P	H	I
		H			N	E	T		T	A	T
E	D	I	T		O	R	I	G	A	M	I
	I	S	H				N				O
	S	T	Y	M	I	E		P	A	I	N
A	H	I		E	L	L		P	I	N	A
		C	O	L	L	A	T	E	R	A	L
		A				L					
G	A	T	E	A	U		L	O	V	E	D
	L	E	A	R	N		E	V	I	T	A
	E	D	U	C	A	T	I	O	N	A	L